"Inside everyone of us is a little dog
and a BIG-Dog. Those of us who master
the mental techniques of controlling our
Dogs, are the ones who leave the field
victorious." - Steve Knight

The information contained in this book is from the author's personal experience and is not intended to replace medical advice.
Use of the information provided is at the sole choice and risk of the reader.

Library of Congress Catalog Control Number: 2004195780
Publisher's Cataloging-in-Publication
(Prepared by Let's Win! Publishing).

Let's Win! Publishing
Portland, OR

WinningSTATE—Baseball: The Players' Guide to Competitive Confidence
/ by Steve Knight—1st ed.

p. cm.
ISBN: 0-9765361-0-2

1. Sports 2. Psychology
l. Knight, Steve ll. Title.

PRINTED IN THE UNITED STATES OF AMERICA

Baseball

The Players' Guide
to Competitive Confidence

Steve **K**night

Lets Win!
Publishing

TABLE OF CONTENTS

WinningSTATE–Baseball

Charts

Interviews – Teams

Interviews – Players

PREFACE

I entered my first weightlifting tournament in 1974. I barely knew how to perform the lifts and knew nothing about the process of a tournament—I was totally in the dark about competing. My only previous sports experience had been Little League baseball.

I placed last, but survived the inaugural tournament, and then went on to spend eleven years as a competitive weightlifter. I won several state and two national championships, and set an Oregon state record in the Squat at 722 pounds—in 1982—that still stands today. I lifted in the 181-pound weight class.

While conducting numerous seminars across the country on competing and strength training, I invariably get asked how I mentally prepared for the big lifts, and how I kept it together at the big tournaments. Those are tough questions to answer meaningfully in a seminar setting, and there aren't very many books or videos to recommend on how to prepare mentally for competition.

Due to that lack of resources, and remembering my own confusion during the pre-national (rookie) years, I often wondered how a book on developing the mental skills of a competitor would be received.

In the fall of 2001 I decided to write *WinningSTATE-Wrestling*: A how-to book on systematically constructing a tournament mindset, and how to focus an athlete's most powerful weapon—his mind. My core objective was/is to help athletes in all sports better understand the mental side of competing, so they can execute at a higher level.

WinningSTATE-Wrestling has been so well received; I decided to adapt my stadium management routines and confidence building techniques specifically for baseball players.

Here's to the BIG-Dog deep inside us all.

Let's Win!

ACKNOWLEDGEMENTS

As I look back over months of preparation many individuals come to mind that influenced the outcome of this book.

Before acknowledging a few special contributors, with tremendous gratitude I must thank the coaches and players who appear in the "Interviews" section. Gathering the requested info and photos was a chore for all, and I sincerely appreciate your efforts. Thank you!

To ALL the photographers, your photos make this book come alive.

To Robert Neiman: Thank you for giving us permission to use your incredible art on the cover. Go to neiman-posters.com

To my son Nick: Thanks for your contribution—you have a great sense of simple—keep up the good work.

To Ian Jones: Thanks for your editing and attention to detail.

To Dan Frost: Thanks for grappling with the concepts; your unique vision definitely added to the clarity and impact of this presentation.

To Nick Bahr: Great job with the website. Thanks.

To Anthony Maggio: Awesome job producing the interviews, and many thanks for your contributions during layout.

To my friend Kim Ross: Your initial encouragement was invaluable. Thanks so much for your many hours, your energy, and your genuine interest in this project.

Finally, to Jody, Dan, and the new addition to our family: Yeah Baby! (more appropriate than ever). Thanks … always … for your love and caring.

DEDICATION

To my first coach: Honestly, I don't think I would have made it through the confusion at that pivotal time in my young life without your influence, direction, and unselfish involvement. Thank you. Forever, you will be at the top of my impact list.

Many of the concepts you shared and taught are at the core of this book. This is for you.

INTRODUCTION

WinningSTATE-Baseball is the first of its kind; the first book to break down in simplistic form the mental side of competing. Within these chapters you're going to learn how-to successfully battle the natural ups-and-downs of insecurity and self-doubt; you're going to learn how to focus your mind and to believe in your physical abilities; ultimately, you're going to develop the confidence and composure of a veteran competitor.

I have attended hundreds of sporting events over my thirty-year athletic career, and what never ceases to amaze me is the number of athletes who suffer defeat because they aren't prepared—mentally.

I've seen distracted, fearful minds, coupled with disorganized approaches to games and tournaments—leave thousands of great athletes sitting in dejection and bewilderment after losing a major competition that they should have won. To win games, to be a champion at any level, an athlete needs two sets of skills: the physical skills of his sport, and the mental skills of a competitor. This is why I've written this book.

The world-class techniques, methods, and routines I present can be applied to all sports, but this edition of *WinningSTATE* is specifically for baseball players of all styles and ages, who want to take their competitive skills to a winning level.

As a former state and national Powerlifting champion I'm familiar with hard work, but playing baseball requires a physical skill-set that is way beyond hard work; it requires quick judgment, hand-eye coordination, and split-second timing that is extraordinary. Then, in a game setting, add to the picture the intense pressure to win, a packed stadium, and heightened emotions to make the big play or drive in the winning run, and the need to have the mental skills of a seasoned competitor becomes crystal clear.

I've watched countless stud athletes over the years endure the commitment to practice required for high-level sports, only to go to games and fall apart, or "lay-an-egg" as a friend of mine would say. All to often too many great ball players crumble mentally and lose long before they ever set foot on the field or step into the batters box—I call this a confidence meltdown.

A meltdown is painful to watch because these same dazed, doubt-dominated athletes would be fearless players, if they had a second set of skills: the mental skills of a competitor.

INTRODUCTION CON'T

Let me ask you, what's the point of perfecting a pro cut, if you're too nervous to swing? What's the point of developing high-level physical skills, if mentally you're a weak competitor? It's pointless, unless practice is the only reason you're out for the sport, which I doubt is the case for most of you; most of you want to compete.

My passion for writing this book is to help baseball players of all ages find their BIG-Dog that lives deep inside. My hope is that WinningSTATE will not only be visually entertaining and competitively inspiring, but also an extremely powerful competitive tool for players, coaches, and parents alike. My goal is to help players become champions, and to help rookies get their first "clutch" hit.

As a competitor, other than winning, the most gratifying feeling is knowing that as you faced the pressure you didn't flinch. Win or lose you know, you rose to the occasion and competed. Win or lose, when the final inning is over, you're able say to yourself truthfully: "I didn't choke. I gave it all I had."

Study the techniques and routines in the following chapters to take your mental skills to the next level, find your BIG-Dog and believe in yourself, so you can deliver the level of play you dream of—clutch, game winning play.

Here's to believing,

Steve Knight
Author
WinningSTATE–Baseball

"Steve Knight is one of the few American Powerlifters who displays the mental control and confidence of the European Olympic Lifters."

Bill Starr, Author
Defying Gravity—How To Win At Weightlifting

Winning
STATE™

Baseball

Lets Win!

Publishing

Chapter One

WINNING • A Game Mindset

You know how to play the game. You've worked hard at practice. You know the right place to be on defense. Your hitting game is strong, your throwing game is right on target and you know what you're capable of. You've dreamed about ripping the game winning homer, pitching the flawless post-season shutout or diving to grab the impossible out. But instead, when the pressure is on, you've choked at the plate, committed errors or released wild throws. Too many times you've ended up walking off the field feeling disappointed and dejected, knowing you could've played a better game; you wonder why you didn't have your best game when you needed it the most. You wonder what's missing. You wonder why the last game of the season has never been your best. You wonder how you can take it to the next level. Answer: It's time to learn how to compete.

"We are what we repeatedly do. Excellence, then, is not an act, but a habit."

— Aristotle

Above: Seton Hall Prep second baseman (2003) Ryan Clark waits for a throw to tag out the runner. Photo: Seton Hall Prep Acacdemy.

Left Page: J.D. Closser, fifth round draft pick for the Arizona Diamondbacks 1998, makes the tag while playing in the Pioneer Baseball League, Missoula Montana. Photo: Kyle Clapman.

Games and tournaments are entirely unlike practice. The excitement, the strange environment, the players you've never faced before, freaked-out teammates and the tremendous pressure to win all require mental skills that have to be developed, just like hitting, fielding, running and throwing. Physically, most athletes train their butts off, but mentally do very little to prepare for competition. *WinningSTATE-Baseball* focuses on the mental skills clutch players use in pressure situations to consistently perform at a high-level.

WinningSTATE-Baseball explains the fundamentals of thinking like a competitor. I talk about what drives a champion, the difference between practice and competition, and how to mentally approach games ready to compete. I outline how to develop a focused game mindset, which will take your competitive skills to the next level and will instantly improve game performance—guaranteed.

Jon Edmondson (throwing), of Hope College attempts to complete a double play, while Albion's Mike Pish tries to break up the play. Photo: Sentinel/Brian Forde.

Oakton High School (Vienna, Virginia) wins the 2003 Virginia state baseball championships. Photo: Dean Hoffmeyer for Richmond Times-Dispatch.

The Stadium

Being at an unfamiliar ballpark in an unfamiliar city with huge crowds and all kinds of distractions can be overwhelming to say the least. It can shatter your concentration if you don't have the mental skills of a competitor.

Chapter 2, The Stadium: Conquer It, will show you how to effectively deal with the intensity of the stadium environment. Chapter 2 will teach you the technique of narrowing your thinking to just five physical places in the building—your Game Posts—and it will also teach you seven primary Game Routines. Combined, these techniques and routines will bring the typically unpredictable, chaotic environment at games and tournaments under control. You'll learn how to ignore distractions, stay focused, and ultimately, you're going to learn how to conquer the Stadium.

Nutrition

Nutrition is often an undervalued aspect of non weight-cutting sports. If your goal is to be a consistent Player, especially at multi-day tournaments, nutrition is significant. To compete on a superior level our bodies need clean-burning, high-octane, quick-recovery fuel—not weak, low-energy tongue food: candy, plastic cheese, hot dogs, and colored sugar water.

"You wonder how you can take it to the next level. Answer: It's time to learn how to compete."

Chapter 3, Nutrition: Game Fuel, will show you how tournament nutrition is not about eating—it's about fueling.

Attitude

Attitude is what makes a champion—not a perfect swing or an awesome glove. Attitude is the glue that brings all of the physical and mental training together. As competitors we live or die by attitude.

Inside every one of us are a little dog and a BIG-Dog. What makes some of us more little dog than BIG are personality type, genetics, and environmental factors. But mostly it's genetic—some puppies bite, and some puppies don't. The question is: Can passive puppies learn to be aggressive dogs?

Chapter 4, Attitude: Game Mode, will help you understand where you fit on the Dog Scale, but most importantly, little dogs will learn how to let their BIG-Dog out. BIG-Dogs will learn how to calm themselves down.

Visualization

Next to nutrition, visualization is the most misunderstood aspect of game and tournament competition. Typically, visualization is thought of as "seeing" victory. How is seeing victory going to stop you from wetting yourself before your first trip to the plate or when your team needs a clutch defensive play? Answer: It can't. Chapter 5, BIG-Dog Vision will teach you how to conquer doubt by seeing your confidence, which will help you compete at a higher level, not just stroke your ego.

The Battle

The battle that will make you a champion is fought in your mind, not on the field. The battle is over composure. As the game progresses toward your spot in the line up, emotions surge, then you step-up to the plate and your stomach twists. This is the critical time for many of you. It's when your little dog takes over; you crash and burn mentally, long before the pitch is even thrown.

Chapter 6, The Battle: Composure, will teach you how to stay emotionally balanced and confident during pressure situations, so your BIG-Dog can come out and dominate ... Show some teeth.

Dream

Your dream is your power, and it must be crystal clear. When you're hanging with your friends and it's time for drills or mental preparation exercises, why do you head home to practice? When your team is down two runs in the ninth, and you must dig down deep to manage the pressure, where does the fire come from? When you're

Dominic Ramos, freshman shortstop for Southwest Texas takes the throw as sophomore Eric Schindelwolf of Texas A&M tries to beat the tag. Photo: Stuart Villanueva.

Players unknown. Photo by Wagner Photography, Fort Myers, FL.

Confidence
The Player's Guide

Steps To A Focused Game Mindset:

#1   Game Posts
Coordinate the entire game from 5 physical locations in every stadium: your Game Posts.

#2   Tournament Fuel
Fuel yourself with high-energy carbs and fats, not weak, low-energy tongue food.

#3   Control Your Minds
Claim your confidence and focus your power; decide which of your minds is in control. "I can't or I can!"

#4   Believe
High level performance requires more than physical skills, it requires mental skills as well—you must believe.

#5   Game Mode
Narrow your focus to just the game. Put everything else in life on hold, until after each game moment.

#6   BIG-Dog Vision
Use **BIG-Dog Vision** to compose yourself; turn doubt into confidence by visualizing images when you were "clutch." Insert confident DVD.

#7   Step-Up
In every game, at some point, it comes down to proving yourself. Are you a Player or a faker? Step-Up!

Use *WinningSTATE's* techniques and routines to "think" with a focused game mindset. Block out distractions and tame little dog uncertainty to maintain superior competitive confidence—you must focus and believe.

"The only one who can tell you 'you can't' is you. And you don't have to listen." — Nike

WinningSTATE–Baseball

"As competitors we live or die by attitude."

tempted by friends who are experimenting with dangerous things, who don't care about the threat to your eligibility and want you to go along and partake, why do you say, "Nah, I think I'll pass." Answer: You have a dream. The power to discipline yourself, to make the tough social decisions comes from your dream, and it must be crystal clear. Do you want to distinguish yourself as a champion, or live among the average?

Chapter 7, Dream: Your Power, will help you clearly define your dream. It will help you understand how your dream is your power, and how your dream provides the motivation to stick with your training, and to be the very best you can be—a champion.

Dream BIG, it's your power.

The Mac-n-Seitz Indians dugout. Lenexa, Kansas. Photo: Unknown.

"Nothing can be done without hope and confidence.

— Helen Keller

SUMMARY

- Deliver your best game when you need it most.
- Mentally separate practice from games.
- Narrow your focus to conquer the stadium.
- Think with a Game Mode mindset.
- Find your confidence with BIG-Dog Vision™.
- Control your Dogs to stay composed.
- Dream. Create your power.

"The key elements that transform a player into a competitor is captured in the seven bullets above, so be sure each one makes sense.

"Competing successfully under pressure takes two sets of skills: physical skills and mental skills. When you work your mind, as well as your body, your stats will quickly rise." — Steve Knight

Chapter Two

THE STADIUM • Conquer It

The stadium can present many focus challenges for young athletes: Intense coaches, dugout dynamics, opposing players, and thousands of fans. The distractions are nonstop and the confusion can be overwhelming. The intensity of the stadium will take you out of your comfort zone and leave you numb, babbling in the corner, if you don't have a mental plan.

For many rookies, the immensity of the building, the loud noise, constant visual distractions, and overall game commotion—coupled with extreme emotional instability—makes for an unpredictable roller coaster experience. Simply put, distractions are why many rookies fail to achieve their true competitive potential; they haven't developed the mental skills to ignore distractions and focus on what's important—their confidence.

*"The only place success comes
before work is in the dictionary."*

— Vince Lombardi

Above: Yankee Stadium, built in 1921. A gigantic horseshoe shaped triple-decked ball-park that was the first to be called a stadium—Yankee Stadium. Photo source: Baseball-almanac.com.

Left Page: Harvard players Morgan Brown—pitcher, and Brian Lentz—first baseman, make the play against UMass, Amherst. Photo by Ruby Arguilla for the Harvard Gazette.

Game Mode

If the reason you commit the time, dedication, sacrifice, and hard work is to compete with the BIG-Dogs at the "title" tournaments, your goal should be to show up at state, regionals, and nationals mentally dialed-in, ready to get the most possible out of yourself. Realize that the primary way to deliver consistent, high-level performance is to be mentally prepared, focused, and composed. Plus, being able to remain competitive for long hours, over several days at big tournaments, requires a series of routines that quickly and easily get you into Game Mode: Maximizing concentration and minimizing distractions.

It is vital to make the clear distinction that practice is drastically different from games. When competing, everything should center on maximizing our ability to turn your focus on and off at will. In most sports, it's a hurry-up-and-wait situation; baseball is no exception. Unless you're the pitcher or the catcher, there is a lot of unfocused time between defensive plays, and even if your team is smoking hot at the plate, you'll only get a few at-bats per game. Therefore, having the skills to turn Game Mode on and off is a necessity for high-level "clutch" play.

"Getting horizontal is the key. Our mind and body go into 'rest mode' when we're horizontal."

Third baseman: While this information is vital to all positions, third basemen need to pay extra attention to this point. On the hot corner, you may not get as much action as the shortstop or second baseman, but the balls that come your way usually come much quicker and are hit a lot harder. There is no excuse for being unfocused at any time at third base. If you're going to snag the line drive up the line to save extra bases, you absolutely must have the ability to turn Game Mode on and off with the best of them.

What specifically is Game Mode? It's very serious. And therein lies the problem. Most young athletes don't know how to be serious, which is why we have more posers than players. You can't "act" serious. You're either serious or you're not. Making faces, grunting, and looking all tough isn't serious. Serious to most young athletes is angry or overly emotional. Much of the time when young athletes get real serious they cry, which is understandable, because it's hard to control serious emotions.

Serious is very simple—it's focused. Steely eyed, piercing concentration. No acting, no pretending, no faking, just pure concentration on a specific target. That's serious. That's Game Mode.

Game Mode is about having laser beam focus at specific moments and mentally chilling the rest of the time. Game Mode is about being able to turn on maximum concentration in an instant, and turn it off. Game Mode is having the ability to take your mind to a competitive place, a place that is very different from most other social situations. Game Mode is about competing to win, not just playing for fun.

Over many years of competing on a state and national level, through trial and error, I developed seven Confidence Routines that provide structure and lay the foundation to be able to flip Game Mode on and off at will. They are: Pack It, Fuel It, Rest It, Analyze It, Visualize It, Compose It, and Dominate It.

Unlike emotions, Confidence Routines don't vary from your first play to your last. They are consistent routines that help you create and maintain a focused mindset for crucial times, so you can calm your fears, visualize your strengths, and solidify your confidence. Game Mode is about more than wanting to win; Game Mode is about doing what is necessary to win.

Remember this: We win or lose by believing, and believing is about focus and confidence—focus and confidence is Game Mode.

Arkansa-Little Rock catcher Rick Guarno was picked up by the Colorado Rockies in the fourth round of the 2003 Major League Baseball first—year player draft. Photo by unknown source.

Game Posts

Now that you have a clearer picture of Game Mode, and before we get into the nuts-and-bolts of developing your own personal Confidence Routines, first we need to talk about Game Posts—one of the key perspectives for conquering the stadium.

Picture the stadium where your state tournament is held. See the outside, the concessions area, the huge field, thousands of seats, the scoreboard, the lights, the sounds, the smells … got the picture?

Now, lets narrow your focus to just five physical locations in every stadium, your Game Posts: The Field, The Dugout, On Deck, the Batter's Box, and The Stands. Every game is controlled from those five locations.

Why is narrowing your focus important? Think of a game as if you're walking across a narrow beam high off the ground. What's the first rule? Don't look down. Why? Because looking down will engage your fear and take your concentration off your balance. You'll stumble, fall, and you're dead.

The stadium presents the same kind of challenge. Engaging the commotion always

Game Posts
Maximize Concentration

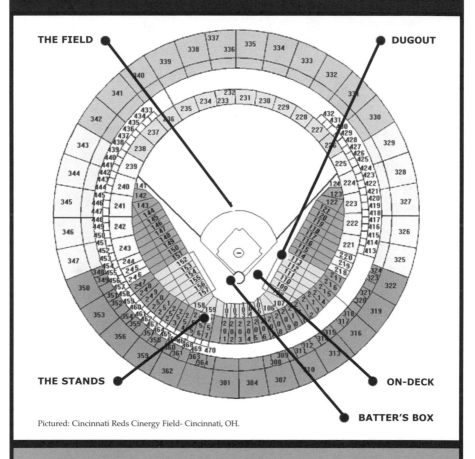

THE FIELD

DUGOUT

THE STANDS

ON-DECK

BATTER'S BOX

Pictured: Cincinnati Reds Cinergy Field- Cincinnati, OH.

Narrow your focus to five physical locations in every stadium: your Game Posts. You'll maximize concentration to better manage stadium intensity, increasing your ability to deliver focused play.

Winning
STATE™
Baseball

Diving to beat the tag is a player from Nebraska Wesleyan University baseball 2003. Photographer unknown.

going on somewhere in the stadium puts you inside the commotion and the commotion inside of you. It's distracting and takes focus away from getting ready to compete.

Our minds can only do one thing at a time; we're either mentally scattered, wandering around the stadium in little dog faker mode—or we're mentally focused, preparing for battle in BIG-Dog Player Mode.

The Field: Remember, our object is to narrow our thinking so we can focus on our confidence. This Game Post (the Field) is not about your position and its defensive requirements; it's about familiarity with that location on any field in the country.

Why? Because you can count on knowing what's up wherever you go—no mystery. Left field is left field. Yeah, the grass might be a little different, and the fence a little farther back or higher, but basically it's the same. Yes, you'll need to make some visual adjustments the first time you walk on to a new field, but once you compare similarities to your home field, adjust your thinking to claiming that spot, you own it. So mentally you can treat your defensive position in any stadium in the country as if it were your home field.

The more mentally comfortable you are with your defensive physical space, the more you'll be able to execute high-level play.

The Dugout: Wow! Dugout dynamics. This is one of the fascinating aspects of competing as a baseball player. Usually in the dugout you're sandwiched between teammates, which can make preparing for your next at-bat difficult, especially if your teammates are distracted or freaked out. Their unstable mindset can affect you if you haven't developed a way to narrow your thinking to concentrate on your confidence.

Tournament Play
Between-Game Sequence

Tournaments are the *critical time*. It's when you and your team win or lose the big championships. Tournament time is when you need between-game routines to help you recover and refocus your competitive mind.

Follow the between-game routines precisely and completely.

Resting: After each game mentally disconnect from the environment. Lie down and close your eyes. *Get horizontal*.

Waking: 20—45 minutes before each game, start moving around and reconnecting with the environment.

Stretching: As you're waking, drink some fluid and go through a brief stretching routine. Mentally get ready to start preparing yourself to control your competitive minds.

Organizing: As you near the start of the next game, gather your gear and other BIG-Dog necessities.

Game Mode: It's time. Narrow your focus and believe!

"If winning isn't everything, why do they keep score?"

— Vince Lombardi

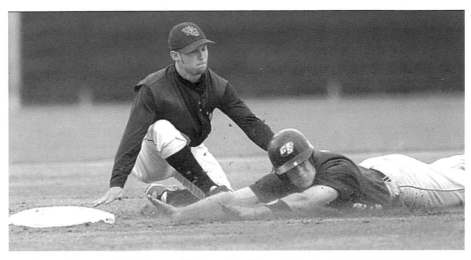

Second baseman Todd Roper of Western Carolina puts the tag on Georgia Southern's Brendan Gilligan. Photo by Mark Haskett

Fakers will be grabbing hold of everyone around them because they're scared to death and need reassurance. Those of you who want to deliver clutch play need to have routines that you use to get your mind right as your position in the lineup approaches. We'll talk more about these routines in Chapter 4.

On Deck: You're almost up and your emotions surge. You've been studying that pitcher who has a mean slider, which is a difficult pitch for you to hit. You can see yourself ripping a line drive down the third base line, but then BAM! The next vision is walking back to the dugout dragging your bat in dejection after that pitcher got you with that slider.

On Deck is where we use the Meltdown Meter to keep close watch on our confidence level. Are we solid or coming apart? Here is where we drastically narrow our thinking and start to think about what we want to do versus what we don't want to do. On Deck is where most of us flip the switch from chilling to Game Mode.

The Batter's Box: A 3' by 6' area is where it all happens; most careers are made or lost in the batter's box. What's weird is different circumstances surround each at-bat. Sometimes you just need to get on base, other times your team needs a sacrifice, other times you'll need to rip one into the outfield to drive in a run, and still other times you need a homer to tie the game. But guess what, even though all those circumstances are different, your swing and mindset stay the same. What's my point? Getting mentally involved with all of those external circumstances are a distraction. Tune into what Coach wants you to do, and then narrow your thinking to your confidence and your swing. A confident, no-hesitation swing will make solid contact and the rest will be history.

The Stands: Before league games, or at multi-day tournaments, the Stands are where you prepare your competitive minds. All too often, especially for young athletes away from home, the stands represent time to have fun, which isn't bad thing as

Devin Boysen of the North Thurston Jr. Legion team (Matt Chubb/Manager) in Lacey, Washington, pitches against the Olympic Jr. Legion team from Bremerton, Washington. Photo by Denny Brooks / ontherun.com.

long as you don't lose perspective. You're there to compete, not fool around.

The Stands are a place to collect yourself, make mental adjustments, refuel, rest and prepare yourself for the next game. We'll discuss The Stands further in Chapter 4.

Confidence Routines

The seven primary Confidence Routines are actually two pre-game confidence routines and five in-game confidence routines. Follow these routines before, during, and after each game.

Pack-It: On game day, or before you leave for a multi-day away tournament, packing your game necessities is critical. First, make a list. Then make sure ALL of your physical necessities are gathered together and ready to be packed: equipment, clothes, food, and fluids. Pack for each game. Example: If you want a fresh tee-shirt after each game, list it and pack it. If you want a couple of different sweats, put them on the list and pack them. If you have specific music that you want along, list it and pack it.

"One important key to success is self-confidence."

— Arthur Ashe

"Game Mode is about having laser-beam focus at specific moments and mentally chilling the rest of the time."

Whatever is important to you, list it and pack it.

Why put out the extra effort to make a list? Because when there are a lot of things to organize and you don't want to leave anything behind, a list provides assurance. Little dogs: Your mother is not your list—do it yourself.

Don't pack your bag(s) until you've gathered everything in a group on the floor in front of you and you can check it off before you pack it. Be organized and meticulous about packing your necessities. Not only will you have everything you want and need at the game or tournament, organization puts your mind in a calm, focused place—a game frame of mind.

I strongly suggest bringing a sleeping bag or large blanket and a headrest of some sort to away tournaments. The sleeping bag is not for getting into. It's for padding. Bleachers or the stadium floor aren't the most comfortable surfaces.

Make yourself as comfortable as possible between games. Your recovery and mental freshness will be that much better when you're able to lie down, close your eyes, and disconnect periodically—even if it's just for a few minutes.

Fuel-It: If you're a junk-food eater and a colored sugar-water drinker, study Chapter 3 with heightened interest. The Fuel & Hydration Routine is one of the KEY routines to ensuring your competitive advantage.

"Rest-It": Resting is less for your body and more for your mind and emotions. The psychological intensity of maintaining composure during the final thirty minutes before a game and the emotional ups and downs of the game itself are very draining, and require mental regrouping. To repeat: Resting is less for your body and more for your mind and emotions.

Getting horizontal is the key. Our body and mind go into "rest mode" when we're horizontal. So after each game, fuel and hydrate, then lie down, close your eyes and chill. Ideally, you want to fall asleep for 10, 20 or 30 minutes, then wake up with that thick head feeling. That's when you know that you've done all you can to recharge your mental battery.

Sitting up and mentally engaging the tournament is better than running around. But, remember when you're sitting up you're only partially recovering, and partially refocusing your competitive mind.

For optimal rest and recovery, do your best to get horizontal.

Analyze-It: Clutch play isn't about luck; it's about presence of mind. One of the factors is analyzing the variables of the game so you can make solid decisions. From a hitting perspective you want to be analyzing the pitcher: rhythm, speed, types of pitches, etc. Defensively you're thinking about your strengths and key plays your team has been working on. Mentally have a routine you automatically use to continuously analyze the variables of the game. This isn't a laser beam focus like Game

Mode; it's more like being mentally present vs. daydreaming about your girlfriend, or what you and your buddies are doing after the game. The more you stay mentally engaged in analyzing real-time variables, the better you're going to do.

Visualize-It: Visualization is one of the most important aspects of high-level performance. We've devoted an entire chapter to teaching you BIG-Dog Visualization techniques, so read Chapter Five over and over until you understand the process and can visualize at will. You will use BIG-Dog Visualization techniques constantly.

Compose-It: Confidence comes and goes. It's fleeting—especially as a young athlete. As defensive pressure situations build or as a critical at-bat approaches, your nerves explode. This is where composure skills are vital. Chapter 6 is your guide utilizing the mental skills you're building to stay composed during intense pressure situations.

Dominate-It: This is more of an attitude than it is a routine. Even though there is a mental sequence to go through, you'll find that Game Mode activates itself as a natural result of doing everything else right. Follow me? Let's break it down.

If you're practiced and conditioned, if you understand that competing is more than just playing, if you know how to let your BIG-Dog out, if you're rested, focused, and composed, if you truly believe in yourself no matter the situation, and if you can take that mindset and show some teeth as you face the competition, you're automatically in Game Mode and will dominate whatever is in front of you.

In summary, by narrowing your focus to your five Game Posts and consistently using your Confidence Routines, the stadium and all of its distractions becomes manageable.

Stay Focused

During game and tournament hours there is always something to do. Doing nothing is something. Doing nothing requires discipline. It sounds weird, but doing nothing at critical times makes you a disciplined individual. Why do I point this out? Do the math. During games or multi-day tournaments the amount of potentially unfocused time is far greater than focused time. That is why it is essential to learn the right way to do nothing, so your competitive mind will be ready for each game moment.

Within the "stay focused" category here is one of those ugly topics I have to address—family and girlfriends. Like it or not, both are distractions. Unless family members or girlfriends have competed at a high level they won't understand all that is required to physically and mentally stay on the championship side of the tournament.

It's not their fault. They have good intentions. Hanging out with loved ones

"The world doesn't owe me anything, but it deserves my very best."

— Author Unknown

Palm Beach, Florida: Central High's Aaron O'Connell pitches against Royal Palm Beach High School. Photo by Sun Sentinel staff Mark Randall.

between games can be comforting and soothing. That's not a bad thing. Players need lovin' too.

But, unless you go underground and disconnect so you can fully recover and refocus your competitive mind, you will get caught. All of a sudden your team will be getting ready for your next game, and you won't be prepared—not a good situation to be in at state or nationals.

Interacting with family and friends is OK right after each game when you're fueling and hydrating. But, within fifteen or twenty minutes it's time to get horizontal and go into rest mode—to disconnect and regenerate.

No matter what happens, do your best to stay focused, even if it's just chilling and you're thinking about everything you've been doing right and how you're going to handle yourself during the next game.

At games and tournaments, everything in real life is put on hold. Everything. Nothing matters except for the next out, or your next pitch. Nothing. You have to be selfish during games and tournaments, and your supporters (family and friends) should not only respect that, they should help you be selfish.

Focus totally on your routines, competing, and playing skills. A little game watching isn't bad, but don't get emotionally involved. Save your energy for your matches. The less you engage what is going on around you the more focused you'll be on competing. Control games and tournaments from your five Game Posts, and everything else in life can wait until you're through competing for the day.

If you carefully follow your Confidence Routines you will get to each game focused, confident and ready to compete.

Gear Issues

A key element to keeping your competitive mind focused is learning how to deal with the unexpected. Gear issues can be a little unnerving, even for a seasoned competitor. Leaving something behind, losing it, or having something break can be very distracting, so having a backup gear plan is not only smart, it is essential.

I've seen world-class competitors so emotionally attached to their gear that fellow competitors would purposefully steal or break their gear just to distract them and throw them off balance. It's actually funny to watch a world-class competitor fall apart because he doesn't have his "special" piece of gear.

So, what if your bat breaks? First, don't react like a rookie; it's not that critical, so don't come unglued. Yes, it's your favorite, and it feels the best, and you're the most comfortable with that particular bat. So? It's a bat. Shift gears (no pun intended) and make the necessary adjustments. Know which is your second-string bat, deal with the distraction calmly, make the adjustments, and compete.

If you have specific hats, shirts, music, etc. that are absolutely critical in maintaining your psychological balance, confidence, and competitive frame of mind, you'd better have a plan. Stay organized so you have your lucky things at your fingertips when you need them.

No matter what goes wrong—because undoubtedly things will go wrong—remain composed. You're there to compete. Caring about gear is pure distraction.

Practice During League Play

Practice narrowing your thinking to your Game Posts and using your Confidence Routines during league play, and other local tournaments leading up to state and nationals. The more familiar you are with your Game Posts and Confidence Routines the more focused you'll be at the major title tournaments.

S U M M A R Y

- ◆ Conquer the distractions of the stadium.

- ◆ Narrow your thinking to five universal Game Posts to make every ballpark feel familiar.

- ◆ Be able to turn laser beam focus on and off.

- ◆ Get horizontal to rest and recover.

- ◆ Run through your Confidence Routines many times each game to maintain emotional stability.

- ◆ Don't "act" serious, be serious.

"Recognizing the dangers of the stadium is one of the first steps toward learning how to compete. Whether it's at your local park, your high school field, or a big league stadium, game time distractions can be overwhelming. Narrow your thinking to manage the distractions." — Steve Knight

Chapter Three

NUTRITION • Game Fuel

Essential. Crucial. Vital. Critical. Do I have your attention? Nutrition is extremely important. Other than controlling doubt, I don't know of any other aspect of tournament competition that has greater significance.

One reason nutrition does not get the attention it deserves is because most people haven't played all-out do-or-die, game after game, day after day, and they don't realize how draining tournament competition can be. But as you players know, at the end of a difficult game there's nothing left in the gas tank.

Being able to have laser beam concentration, split second timing, and instant reac-

"The best way to predict the future is to create it."

— Peter F. Drucker

Above: Exton, PA: Pitcher Mike Pigott of Downingtown East High School coached by Russ Wren vs. unknown hitter from West Chester Henderson H.S. Photo by Downtown East Baseball.
Left Page: Naperville, Illinois: North Central College. Photo by Unknown.

tions throughout an entire game, tournament, and post season, can easily make the difference between coming home a champion or coming home a loser. One missed clutched play because you were out of gas can end your season. The importance of having quick, new energy for immediate recovery is crucial.

Catchers: While all ballplayers need to closely follow proper fueling instructions, catchers should pay extra close attention. Think about the end of a game, when your pitcher is struggling and there's a runner on third. The pitcher throws a sinker in the dirt, and you have to react. You've been crouched behind the plate all game. It's hot outside and you've been sweating like crazy under all that heavy gear. But here comes the pitch and you need to stop it. Do you have what you need in your tank to make the quick move to block the ball? What if it gets past you? Do you have the explosion to jump up, drop your mask, and get there before the winning run crosses the plate? If you fuel like a BIG-Dog, you will.

Food Is Fuel

Think of food as more functional than emotional, especially for tournaments. In other words, detach your tongue. Don't just think of what tastes good; think of what your

Tournament Fuel
High-Octane Sources

Fast Burning Carbs:
Fruit - Apple (skinned)
Orange
Banana

Slow Burning Carbs:
Grain - Whole Wheat
Bread
Muffins
Bagels

Long Burning "Good" Fat:
Cream Cheese
String Cheese
Peanut Butter

Carb/Fat Combo:
Bagel & Cream Cheese
Bagel & Peanut Butter
Peanut Butter & Jelly
Nut Mix
Wrap or Sandwich

HYDRATION

70% Water   30% Sports Drinks

Little dogs eat, BIG-Dogs fuel.

Tournament day is not the day to indulge your taste buds, be smart about food and fluids—*detach your tongue.*
Hydrate primarily with water.

Winning STATE
Baseball

Michigan's Brock Koman (10) drops the ball as he tries to tag out Minnesota Gophers Ben Pattee (21) as pitcher Drew Taylor tries to offer help. Photo by Danny Moloshok.

body and mind need to recover and be ready for your next game. Food is just fuel. For optimum tournament performance choose high-octane, quick recovery BIG-Dog fuel over weak, low-energy tongue food. You don't have to become a nutritionist in order to understand the basic differences between BIG-Dog fuel and tongue food. Stay with me here and I'll keep this as simple as possible.

Fuel Sequence
Water + Carbs + Fats

Water + Fruit + Combo + Combo

REAL FOOD is optimum. Combine carbs with a carb/fat combo.

HYDRATE until you need to use the restroom. Hydrate more with water than sports drinks.

Below: Protein options for multi-game tournaments and road trips:

| Grilled Fish/Chicken Pasta/Rice/Veggies | Stuffed Potato | Turkey Sandwich | Chicken Wrap |

Carb/fat combos are the keys to maintaining consistent, high-energy levels on tournament day. *Be smart about food and fluids—detach your tongue.*

Winning STATE™
Baseball

"Optimum tournament fuel and fluids come from nature. They haven't been processed or modified from their original state."

Think of food as two groups: types and sources. Types: proteins, carbs, and fats. Sources: bad, good, and optimum. Blending carbs and fats from optimum sources results in high-octane, quick recovery BIG-Dog fuel.

Proteins

On tournament day, proteins are the least desirable type of food for two reasons: 1) Proteins take longer to digest; 2) The body doesn't use proteins as quick energy. The body uses proteins to rebuild muscle and other cells. It doesn't use protein as gasoline (energy). Between games is not the time to rebuild cells. Between games is the time to fill your empty gas tank.

The primary sources of protein are beef, poultry, and fish. Most state tournaments are multi-day events. Protein is a good thing at night, when you're through playing for the day, but not between games. In fact, you want a little protein at night for a variety of reasons, just not a full belly. A six-ounce can of tuna is perfect. Tuna is easy to digest and won't lay in your stomach, as opposed to beef. A burger is the last thing your body needs during a tournament. Save beef for a victory dinner.

Carbs & Fats

Carbs and fats are the types of food that provide immediately usable energy. Effectively combining carbs and fats is the key to having a huge gas tank.

Think of carbs and fats like the paper, twigs, and logs you would use to build a fire. The paper and twigs are carbs – quick fuel. Fats are the logs – denser, longer burning fuel. Proteins are like green wood that just lies there smoldering.

Split carbs into two categories: simple (paper) and complex (twigs). You want a little of each. Fruit is a simple carb, and the quickest energy to get into your blood stream. The body doesn't have to do anything to fruit sugar in order to burn it.

Grains are complex carbs (twigs) that take your body a little longer to burn. The body has to work a little to digest grains, but grains will provide a longer burning energy stream, as opposed to fruit (paper), poof, gone.

Fats are probably the least understood, and the most important. Your body loves fat because it's concentrated, dense energy. There are twice as many calories (energy) in one gram of fat than there are in one gram of carbs. Fats are truly the logs for your body's furnace.

Some of the misinformation you may have read includes the notion that fat slows digestion. That's incorrect. The right way to look at fat is that it's slower to digest, which is a good thing.

"Don't just think of what tastes good, think of what your mind and body need to recover, and to be ready for your next game."

Example: Think of trying to get a blazing fire going that will last for hours with just paper and twigs. You can't do it. The fire will blaze for about 10 minutes and then it's out. Not even a coal will be left. If you try to run on just carbs, by the end of the game, or the end of the day, you will run out of fuel when you need it most.

Again, the key to building a great fire is a combination of carbs and fats, short-term energy and long-term energy.

Review the high-octane tournament fuel examples, and limit yourself to those choices. Think with BIG-Dog Vision™, not with your tongue, at least in season and for tournaments. Manage your food choices for championship level performance.

Optimum Sources

Optimum tournament fuel and fluids come from nature. They haven't been processed or modified from their original state.

Man-made products, like bars, have been altered—preservatives have been added for longer shelf life, and flavor enhancers added to get your tongue to like it. The processing alters the structure of the food, and makes it harder for your body to burn efficiently. I won't go into how unhealthy processed foods are; I'll just stay focused on their burning capability.

Burgers, fries, and a shake are not optimum tournament fuel sources. The plastic cheese, chips, and hog dogs at the concession stand aren't either.

You can eat cancerous junk all year long if you want to. Yuck! But I encourage you to eat high-octane BIG-Dog fuel during season, and especially at tournaments. Try to look past your taste habits and think of what your mind and body need to recover from the extreme energy drain of games and tournaments.

The key thing to remember—food is fuel—detach your tongue.

First Meal

The first type of food to consume on game day should be a 100 percent real piece of fruit: a banana, orange, or an apple. You know the reason, right? Consume a simple carb (paper) first, which will immediately put fuel in your tank. It will quickly increase your blood sugar level, and you'll feel fueled instantly.

After the initial piece of fruit and water comes a carb/fat combo: A bagel and cream cheese, bagel and peanut butter, or PB&J, plus a nut mix on the side. Stay away from meat.

The amount of carb/fat combo you need depends on your size. If you're less than 150 pounds you may only need one bagel, but if you're more than 200 pounds you may need a couple of them.

The key thing to keep in mind is don't overdo it. Control yourself. Don't make yourself uncomfortable. Then take a break and let your digestive system break down the food. After 20 minutes or so if you're still empty, go back for more, but the second round you can skip the fruit. Go for another carb/fat combo. After you've reached the full line, it's time to take a break. There's probably at least an hour before starting pregame warm-ups, so put on your headphones, calm your mind, GET HORIZONTAL, and let your body absorb the mass quantities while your prepare your mind for battle with BIG-Dog Vision.

Between Games

Between games repeat the first meal process: Piece of fruit, water and a carb/fat combo. It's pretty simple. The only variation is the amount of fuel and fluids. If you had a grueling game in the heat, and you're a sweater, you're going to need more water. If it's cool out and the game was a breeze, you won't need as much. Go by feel. The key thing between games besides fueling is rest. GET HORIZONTAL.

Colored Sugar-Water

This is such an ugly subject. You guys hate this information. Like it or not, colored sugar-water isn't all that, despite what the companies who sell it want you to think. The claim of optimally "replenishing vital electrolytes and nutrients" is all a marketing ploy to get you to buy the drinks.

Our bodies are 70 percent water, not 70 percent sports drink. So when you've sweated a couple of pounds of water, you need to replenish it with water. There is so much garbage in many of the "ades" drinks: dyes, sugar, preservatives, etc., that your body has to work at discarding the garbage in order to use the water left behind.

The refined sugar that is in the "ades" drinks is not ideal; don't buy into the claim that they will help you replenish spent energy faster. Real, unprocessed fruit sugar (already explained) will get in your blood stream faster, and burn better. Don't confuse a piece of fruit with drinking gallons of fruit juice. A large amount of fruit juice is not recommended. It's too acidic and will cause digestive issues. To be very clear, I'm not advocating hydrating with fruit juice. I'm suggesting eating a single piece of fruit after each game to bring your blood sugar level back instantly.

Sodium is not the cure all for getting your electrolytes back in balance either. A simple multi-mineral tablet will do more for replenishing electrolytes and will also help you keep from cramping.

If you choose to use the "ades" drinks because of tongue preference, use them sparingly, and in combination with water, like a 70/30 mix. That is 70 percent water. I'm not talking about mixing them together. I'm saying seven glasses of water to three glasses of sports drink. The only exception is after playing in the extreme heat and you've sweated off pounds of fluids you should stick predominately with water until you get your fluid level back up where it needs to be. Then include some "sports drink" if you can't control your tongue.

One of the real dangers of colored sugar-water, the "ades" drinks, is you become addicted, and won't drink water, so you will fail to hydrate as much as you need to.

"Little dogs focus on taste. BIG-Dogs focus on fuel."

Example: On a multi-game day, if it's in the 90's and you're a big sweater, by the end of the day you'll be totally dehydrated. Why? Do the math: It's easy to sweat 2-3 pounds per game, and if you play 3 games that day, that is 9 pounds of fluid you will need to replenish. You can't get there with colored sugar-water guys; it's too syrupy, and has too much junk in it. Instinctively you'll stop hydrating at about 5 to 7 pounds. Get the mental picture? A monster sports drink container—the big one—is 64 ounces, that's 4 pounds. You'd have to drink at least two of those in a day. You won't do it, so you don't hydrate.

Simply put, hydration is about function, not taste. Taste should not be part of the equation. Little dogs focus on taste, BIG-Dogs focus on fuel. So, little dogs, get over it.

Don't Change A Thing

This may be confusing. I've told you to focus on fuel, not junk. Now I'm telling you don't change a thing. What I mean is if you don't add some natural, high-octane foods to your diet during the week, so that your body can get used to digesting good food, it might not be a good idea to make drastic changes at games or tournaments.

Sometimes a junk digestive system has a hard time with dense energy foods. If you're a Pop-Tart, sugared cereal breakfast eater, a bagel and cream cheese might cause some digestive issues the first couple of times. You want to stay as close to your "standard" food routine as possible; it's what your body knows.

For optimum performance during season add some high-octane tournament fuel to your daily and weekly food intake. This does two things: It will familiarize your body with dense energy foods, and it will help you recover and rebuild more quickly during the week.

Another example of don't change a thing ties to your first meal of the day when you're out-of-town at tournaments. Be careful about going to a restaurant for the "great" breakfast before the "big" day. Emotionally that sounds and feels good, but unless you've eaten the "great" breakfast at that restaurant before, it's not a good idea. Remember, stay with what your body knows. Eating breakfast at an unfamiliar restaurant on tournament day is high risk. You don't know what you're going to get. Plus, just because you've made it to the second round of a tournament doesn't mean it's time to celebrate.

If going to a restaurant is a must, you want to be smart about your choices. Bacon and eggs, hash browns and toast, pancakes, biscuits and gravy; are all tongue and taste habit related choices. Get rid of the bacon; add some fat (real butter) to the pancakes, and who knows about the biscuits and gravy. Personally, on tournament morning I wouldn't even consider going to an unfamiliar restaurant … Not a chance!

Remember, game day is not the day to indulge your taste buds. Save that for after the game, a victory dinner is all-good.

S U M M A R Y

- ◆ Think of food as fuel.
- ◆ Forget taste. Go for nutrition, your mind and body need to recover.
- ◆ Grab fruit for an instant boost.
- ◆ Combine carbs and fats to sustain high energy.
- ◆ Save proteins for after the game to rebuild muscle.
- ◆ Hydrate with water.
- ◆ Detach your tongue. Fuel, don't eat.

"The information and recommendations in this chapter have special meaning, which extend beyond elevating your tournament performance. Choosing what type of food to consume daily: organic vs. processed, is one of life's critical decisions.

"Look around, ask questions, understand that food is about more important things than what we like or dislike. Do yourself good; get interested in understanding the difference between processed tongue food and organic healthy food." — Steve Knight

Chapter Four

ATTITUDE • Game Mode

As competitors, we live or die by attitude.

In the introduction, I mentioned that I've watched numerous stud players lose before they ever set foot on the field. Actually, I've witnessed countless athletes from a wide variety of sports, on all levels, with the same problem. They haven't learned how to control their emotions. Doubt demons dominate their thinking centers and mentally they submit long before the physical competition ever begins.

When athletes experience severe doubt, which I call a "meltdown," they have a certain look—almost a version of shock. Their eyes are glazed, they don't respond well to conversation, and they seem distant. Mentally, they turn into a choker because they haven't learned how to believe in themselves in pressure situations.

Don't Deny It

I've worked with hundreds of athletes over the years concerning how to manage doubt and fear. The bottom line is we don't get anywhere as competitors unless we openly realize that doubt and fear are inevitable. When we truly hunger to win, and then recognize the possibility of losing, doubt and fear are a natural result. For some,

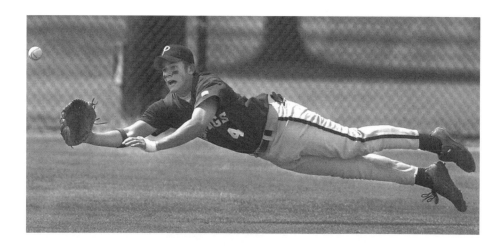

"Keep away from people who try to belittle your ambitions."

— Mark Twain

Above: The real deal—a BIG-Dog. Find your BIG-Dog and show some teeth. Photo: Whole-Dog-Journal.com.

Left Page:Portage Central High School's left fielder DJ Perrin (2003) dives for line drive during a championship game. Photo: Portage Central Baseball.

the fear associated with not knowing the outcome can be paralyzing, but for others the unknown is exciting. Even the most experienced player is going to have moments of doubt and fear; it's natural, so don't deny it. The key to superior performance is learning how to detect – and control – doubt, fear, and intimidation.

For those of you who are thinking, "I never get scared," that's OK; you're either in denial or else winning is not that important to you. Because for those of us who really want to win—when we're up against a strong, worthy opponent and our minds are battling with the possibility of failing—we get scared. Doubt and fear are a reality a competitor has to live with his entire career. Doubt and fear are part of being a player. It's just the way it is.

Player Puppies

Before we get into the process of developing Game Mode mindset, let's go back to the beginning—when we were all puppies.

Realize this: Even the most dominant player was nursed by his mother. Why is this an important point? Because we all start out at the same place—as helpless infants—all of us.

Then, when we begin to grow and our genetics take over; some puppies bite, and some puppies don't. The real question is: Can passive puppies learn to be aggressive dogs?

Answer: Yes they can.

A wolf pack is a good way to illustrate this point. In a pack of 10, there are a couple of BIG-Dogs who constantly duke-it-out for the top position. The middle dogs fight for positions three through seven and the little dogs are reduced to the lower positions in the pack, fighting for the scraps. Those social positions are decided when wolves are puppies, and rarely do those positions change as adults.

This genetic born-to position for a wolf is determined by their inherent size and testosterone level:

Physically Large/aggressive: BIG-Dog
Physically Medium/assertive: Mid dog
Physically Small/submissive: Little dog

It is sooooo important for you middle and little dogs to realize that we humans are very different. We can recognize our "natural" inherent tendencies, and through careful planning and training, we can elevate our basic born-to genetics.

Pay attention here, because if there is one concept I'm trying to express in this book, it's this: For human beings, where we fit on the Dog Scale is up to us.

Those of us who are more naturally the alpha male—the BIG-Dog—probably have a competitive advantage, but only as puppies, because once we human little dogs figure out that being a BIG-Dog is mostly about attitude, a transformation takes place, and we little dogs learn how to show some teeth and let our BIG-Dog out!

Guys … we never earn respect just by winning. We earn respect by fighting, by not swinging with our eyes closed, by giving it our all, by not mentally giving up. It's not about the size of the dog in the fight; it's about the size of the fight in the dog. Will and guts define the size of the fight: swinging with genuine confidence in extreme pressure situations. Determination and guts have nothing to do with physical size,

strength or social position. Guts are about attitude.

No matter where each of our born-to genetics put us on the Dog Scale, little or BIG, to be a winner we have to become more of what we're naturally not. Stay with me here. BIG-Dogs go over the top, and little dogs don't show. BIG-Dogs underestimate their opponents, while little dogs overestimate their opponents BIG-Dogs are shocked when they lose and little dogs are shocked when they win. Both BIG and lit-

Above: Some puppies bite and some puppies don't. Can passive puppies learn to be aggressive dogs? Yes, they can. Photo: Unknown.

Left Page/Left: Mom nursing illustrates that all of us warriors start out at the same place—as helpless babies. Image Source: Unknown. Right: A young BIG-Dog hits the dirt. Photo: RADfoto.

"Some puppies bite, and some puppies don't. The real question is: Can passive puppies learn to be aggressive dogs?"

tle dogs each have detrimental characteristics that require wise, assertive control.

If I had to bet on either a little dog who has learned how to let his BIG-Dog out versus a kid who has been a BIG-Dog all his life, I'll take the little dog any day. The little dog has something more to prove, the need is deeper and fiercer. The majority of the time an "underdog" is a little dog with an attitude, who is going to bleed to the end. Now that's how we earn respect: Take an arrow in the forehead, but never in the back. You all know what this is about, take a catcher for example: A runner is bearing down on home plate, the throw is on the money, he knows he's going to get run over; does he close his eyes, wince, and hope, or stare the runner down, protect the plate, and make the tag? That's attitude, nothing else. Every position has similar "attitude" situations, which translate into the big plays. Guys … attitude and focus win games, not just technique.

I hope you little dogs get this point. The only reason you're a little dog is because you think you're a little dog. All of us, every single one of us has a BIG-Dog deep inside, we just have to find him, and learn how to let him out! When little dogs learn to see life through BIG-Dog Vision everything changes.

Welcome It

The first step in developing a Game Mode mindset is welcoming doubt and fear and then recognizing when you're going into a mental meltdown. Welcome the butterflies and the doubt, step back, breathe, and resurrect those positive BIG-Dog images you've been visualizing just for this moment. Get yourself back to that centered, confident frame of mind—a game mindset.

Personal story: In 1983, I was competing in the US Senior National Powerlifting Championships, which at the time was the most competitive tournament of the year; in fact, even more competitive than the world championships.

I was in the best shape of my career. In a Powerlifting competition the squat is the first lift. I was going to attempt a personal record, which at the time was only a few pounds off a world record. You get three attempts; the first two are basically warm-ups. My first attempt at 644 pounds was easy. My second at 683 pounds was incredibly solid. I felt great. I picked 722 pounds for my third and final attempt. I lifted in the 181-pound weight class. I was up, and in Powerlifting when your name is called you have three minutes to get the weight out of the rack or you're disqualified.

Nationals were being held in a huge arena with a few thousand people attending. As I walked on and took control of the platform I was in a great place mentally. I was totally confident, or so I thought.

Like humans, wolves have many sides to their personalities. Being able to switch from affection to fierce dominance—in an instant—is a necessity for both a wolf, and a competitor.

As I reached the bar and took hold a little voice from demon land said, "Your going to fail," and instantly I got this mental picture of taking the weight out of the rack, my legs breaking off at the knees, and the weight driving me straight down through the platform.

This obviously broke my concentration. I looked up and actually laughed out loud. It startled me and it came from nowhere. I backed away from the weight, took a couple of deep breaths, told the little demon voice where to go and brought back the feelings of my solid warm-ups, memories of successful "big" lifts in the past, and approached the bar for a second time. Doubt resurfaced slightly, but mentally I was full of confidence and plowed ahead.

I made the lift, and in doing so set an Oregon state record that still stands today.

What's the moral of the story? Doubt and fear will surface at the worst possible time. Have the mental skills and composure to look doubt square in the face, conquer it and execute.

Detect It

First, I have to acknowledge that a baseball player's doubt intensity is unique, especially at the plate. The variables are extreme. Various pitchers, complex game situations, and "team" emotions are different than, for example: A weightlifter or an ice skater. I'm not taking anything away from those other athletes, especially since I was one of them; I'm just being real.

Think about it. As a weightlifter I always knew who my opponent was, no confusion, no gray area. 700 pounds is 700 pounds whether it's in New York, Los Angeles, or Tokyo. 700 pounds can't convince itself to be 900 pounds.

An ice skater has a similar situation. Yeah, the ice is different from arena to arena, but the difference is not that significant. The ice is not going to jump up and slam the skater down. The weightlifter and ice skater's doubt demons are very different than a baseball player's.

A baseball player's doubt and intimidation is magnified significantly because he looks a live competitor directly in the eyes. A baseball player's opponent is truly unknown, and it's alive. Even if a player has met a particular pitcher many times before, it's still an unknown. A baseball player has to master doubt and fear or his opponent will blow one right past him.

A baseball player has to work hard mentally at keeping himself centered and confident. That's why it's so important to be skilled at dealing with all of the distractions in game situations and at major tournaments. All who have competed in intense game situations know that you have your hands full with your own emotions and the natural ups and downs of insecurity and self-doubt. So doing everything possible to put yourself in the right place emotionally is what will help you deliver consistent, superior play.

Back to the process. The first step in managing doubt and fear is learning how to detect a meltdown before we reach the critical point, which is easy to do if we're real with ourselves.

When we feel dominant, doubt and fear are not an issue. It's when we feel inferior or uncertain that doubt and fear become major factors. And it's completely natural. When something triggers feelings of insecurity, our two competitive minds, "I can't vs. I can," go into the confidence battle. We flip-flop back and forth from confident to doubtful, especially when the pressure is on and we really want to succeed. But, keep in mind that pressure in itself is not the trigger. It's something else, because in a pressure situation if we're up against a pitcher we know we can hit, we're licking our chops for the opportunity to shine and thinking, "bring it on." Doubt triggers are usu-

Second baseman Nate Reyes (no. 11) of West Ottawa tags out Hamilton's Aaron Lowe (no. 5) for the out. Photo by Sentinel/Brian Forde.

ally intimidation based, and then when pressure is added, BAM! We go into a meltdown.

Detecting doubt is as simple as identifying any other emotion. We know when we're happy, sad, or angry. Doubt is no different. The problem is, when it comes to doubt, we hide from the truth. The first step, as expressed previously, is don't deny it. Be truthful, and say to yourself, "I'm nervous." Laugh it off, and talk yourself down.

Talking Yourself Down

When doubt and fear have you by the throat it's like committing competitive suicide because you're doing it to yourself—you're a "jumper." After you know how to easily detect a meltdown, the next step is to recover by talking yourself down. The process is simple to understand, but hard to do.

To calm ourselves down we have to take our minds to a different place. Whatever we were focusing on to make ourselves feel inferior, we need to disconnect that line of thinking. As previously mentioned meltdown triggers are either the pitcher throws stuff that's hard to hit, or he's beat us in the past, or, and this is the weirdest—he just shut down the best hitter on our team, so we think we can't hit him.

The trick to disconnecting the inferior line of thinking is to force our minds to think about actual, real experiences when we were clutch. It doesn't matter when; they just need to be real experiences we can "believe" in. The key is to make our mind go where we want it to go, because fear is all in our mind. As I've tried to express several times, the battle that will makes us champions is fought in our mind, not on the field. And

Meltdown Meter
BIG-Dog Detector

10.0   RED ALERT, major meltdown, little dogs just wet themselves–all confidence gone.

7.5   Extreme panic, partial meltdown, crumbling.

5.0   Threshold of losing it.

4.0   Genuine doubt, panic.

3.5   Tweaked, but manageable.

3.0   Slightly tweaked.

2.0   Uncertain–composed–BIG-Dog.

1.0   Butterflies–composed–BIG Dog.

0.0   Calm–composed–BIG-Dog.

Doubt is inevitable. Denying it is fatal. To prevent a major meltdown develop the mental skills that detect and control feelings of uncertainty.

First, when you're tweaking, be truthful, don't pretend you're not. If you go into a meltdown use your **BIG-Dog Vision** to recover.

Winning
STATE™
Baseball

those who believe ... win. A great president once said, "The only thing we have to fear is fear itself."

This process of welcoming, detecting, and controlling doubt is presented in much greater detail in Chapter 5. You're going to learn how to see life through BIG-Dog Vision.

Personal story: A couple of years ago when my youngest son was wrestling in high school I traveled with his team to the Reno Tournament of Champions. Most of you baseball players won't be familiar with it, but Reno is one of the most prestigious national wrestling tournaments of the season. The level of talent is seriously deep in every weight class. Remember, the techniques I'm teaching you are for all sports, actually, they're for all of life's pressure situations, so in the following story pay attention to the emotional roller coaster this athlete went through.

My son's team had a couple of wrestlers who, if they showed up emotionally, had the potential to place or win.

I was sort of the team mom. I shuttled the team back and forth from the hotel, kept the tournament fuel flowing, and helped the coaches and athletes with whatever they needed. A lot of the team were rookies at a tournament of that size, and didn't win a match. But, a couple of our guys made it to the medal rounds.

One of our middleweights—152 lbs—whom I'll call "Our Guy" was wrestling for third/fourth. I was chilling in the stands watching the competition as the lighter weight classes started, when Our Guy came up and asked if I'd seen the coaches. He didn't look good—sort of clammy and grayish. I thought to myself, "Oh man, he's going into a meltdown." I told him I didn't know where the coaches were and he took off.

A couple of minutes later he came back and was having problems with a kneepad. The kneepad really wasn't a problem of any significance, but when you're in a meltdown everything is catastrophic. In the middle of telling me about the kneepad he turned and took off. He was coming unglued.

I went and found the coaches on the arena floor and told them that Our Guy was coming apart. They really didn't know what to do. "What does he need," they asked?

I told them he was talking about a kneepad problem, but actually he was just getting twisted about his match. Even though these coaches had numerous first-hand experiences with "tweaked" athletes, they really didn't know how to recognize a meltdown, nor did they have the experience in talking someone down, and then back up to competitive confidence.

Right about then Our Guy found us on the arena floor. He told the coaches about his kneepad issues, and one coach went off to find him another kneepad. One of the other coaches said, "You'll be fine," and that was going to be the end of it. This kid was ready to throw up. Respectfully, I told the head coach (who is an awesome man) that Our Guy needed to be talked down and asked if I could work with him. I got the green light, and asked Our Guy to go for a walk. I put my arm around his shoulder, and as we walked to the other end of the arena, I asked him, "Do you like homework?" He looked at me and could barely get the answer out, "No, not really." "Got a girl friend?" "Yeah." "You like to go fishing?" "What?" he asked. "What about cars?

Game Mode
Narrow Your Focus

Game Mode is about narrowing your focus to block out distractions and stabilize your confidence, so you capitalize on opportunities when the spotlights are on.

Little Leaguers: You're not in the sandbox anymore; it's not time to be nice; and you don't have to share. **Rip it!**

Oliver Dobrian of the Aliso Viejo Diamondbacks at bat. Photo by All-League Sports Photos in Foothill Ranch, CA.

"Baseball is 90% mental, the other half is physical."

— Yogi Berra

You like cars?" I just started asking random questions. He got really confused, but as we talked about absolutely nothing, reality started creeping back in. The random real world questions were disengaging his fear. It's fascinating to watch someone's mind come back from extreme lost-in-fear mode.

Once I started to see his eyes clear and his mind calm down, I asked him why his opponent was in his kitchen. He got a little grin. "Because he beat me yesterday in the semi's." With that statement, Our Guy saw his fear and was then able to be real with himself. Keep in mind that whoever won the upcoming match would receive All American status. Placing at Reno was a BIG deal nationally. You got ink in national papers and magazines, which only helps one's college prospects.

"So basically you can't win," I said. "No, I can win," he snapped right back. "How?" I asked with a whatever kind of a tone. Our Guy stared listing his opponent's strengths and weaknesses; he relived the match from the day before out loud. By the end of his description he was amused at why he was so shook. "I can beat this kid," he said with some conviction. I laughed, slapped him on the shoulder and said, "Exactly." We went back over those thoughts and mental images several times. I told Our Guy he needed to keep his mind right where it was: On his strengths, and his opponent's weaknesses.

A few minutes later Our Guy was back on Earth, with solid competitive confidence, and looking forward to kicking some butt. He laid around chilling until it was time to get into his pre-match warm-ups. He was in a great place mentally and had a totally different look and feel.

Our Guy wrestled a dominant match and pinned his archrival in the third period. It was an exciting match to watch. Our Guy's an All American.

The story continues.

Those two met again twice before state at other tournaments. Our Guy beat his rival soundly both times. Our Guy owned him, or so it seemed.

At state Our Guy was ranked No. 1 and his rival was ranked No. 2. The rankings played out, and they were in the finals. This was going to be an awesome match; we all fully expected, of course, that Our Guy would emerge state champion.

I was not in the trenches with the team at state, so I watched from the stands. As the match began, I could see within seconds that Our Guy was twisted. He opened tentatively and was on his heels. Our Guy's rival was tentative also, having been beaten three times in the previous two months, but once he realized that Our Guy was uncertain, he gained a huge amount of confidence and turned it on. If you know what you're looking for you can see it on video.

In the second period Our Guy rolled his ankle, and did his best to recover, but didn't. His rival hung on and defended well in the third period to become state champion. What a year.

Our Guy owned his opponent, but his doubt let his rival back in the game. And the worst thing is all that doubt was pure fantasy, because he had beaten his rival three times previously under tremendous pressure.

All of you have seen or lived a story like this and it is so important to realize it's all in your mind.

Shortstops: As stated above, the mental aspect here relates to all sports and life in general. But I'm sure many of you can relate to that one hitter who came up early in the game and absolutely smoked a grounder right at you. When that guy comes to the plate with a runner on first and one out in the ninth, you must stay focused on your strengths, not the strength (literally) of your opponent. If you're busy thinking about how hard that monster can hit the ball, how can you expect to stop the next rocket grounder that comes at you? Stay focused on your superior skills, your confidence, and your ability to make the tough play on a hard hit ball in the hole. Confidently do your part in the double play to end the game and preserve the win.

Composure

Once you've learned how to welcome and detect doubt and fear, and then how to talk yourself down, you'll gain a tremendous amount of confidence in the process because your mind and emotions will be focused on your strengths. The more skilled you become at the process of detection and control, the easier it will be to stay confident. The dramatic flip-flopping form confident to doubtful will be less intense, because you'll be ready for doubt and fear to creep up when your opponent is formidable or there is a title on the line. You'll be looking for it, and mentally equipped to control and channel it.

Competing is about composure. When we're composed, we're not lost in that inner land of self-doubt. When we're confident and involved with the external, outer environment, we automatically see the cracks in our opponent's armor, which is where we need to be if we're going to leave the battlefield with our head still connected to our neck.

I encourage you to read the "Interviews Section" in the last part of the book. Pay close attention to each of the champion's descriptions of their Best Moment in Baseball, and their Most Clutch Moment of All Time. It's quite interesting. Almost every one occurred when they were not supposed to win; when they were in the championship game for the big title and they pulled it off by believing in themselves. I didn't ask these champions to describe a game when they were an underdog. I just asked them to describe their Clutch Moment of All Time, and why.

Of course it makes sense: The time they rose to the occasion, conquered their fears, competed and cracked one out of the park, are the times they're most proud of. And they should be. That's what competing is all about: maintaining confidence and composure under extreme pressure and executing.

It's a tremendous personal accomplishment when we can maintain composure under tremendous pressure. Most of the time we're not as outmatched as we think we are. Most of the time the pitcher isn't as good as we think he is. Yes, sometimes we do find ourselves up against someone who is going to blow one by us no matter how well

Players battle for position. Photo: Augusta Chronicle.

we execute. They just have more experience. But the majority of the time we give our opponents way more credit than they deserve.

So what do you do when you're up against someone who has the edge? Stay composed and learn something. If you go into battle a mental midget you won't learn a thing. You accept defeat, which reinforces a little dog mentality. Not good. This is when you can practice controlling your mind by controlling and channeling your doubts and fears. This is something that always amazes me about athletes; if you're truly outmatched, why get shook? Why not go out there and surprise both your opponent and yourself? Go swing and show your opponent you're a competitor. You have nothing to lose and everything to gain.

Game Mode

Now the transformation begins. Once you learn how to detect and control your emotions you can transform from a mere player into a tournament warrior, and it truly is a transformation. The transformation is completely based on believing in yourself.

A true warrior doesn't care if his adversary can throw a 95-mile an hour fastball or a change-up that leaves you guessing. A true warrior is going to suck it up and make solid contact. It's like breaking boards in martial arts. A beginning student can't even break one board. Then, in a short time, he can break three, then five, then seven. What

Midwest City, OK: Tulsa Patriots catcher get a late throw against Perry Diamondbacks runner Hayden Workman at the 13 & Under Super Series National Qualifier (4.18.04). Diamondbacks are coached by Kevin Wilda. Photo by Teri James.

happens? The student not only learns better physical techniques, like using his hips and striking the board square, but more importantly the student learns how to believe and penetrate—to strike through the board.

Those lessons totally apply to a baseball player. Effective play is about penetration—to swing confidently through the pitch, not just to swing at it, but to actually make a pro cut. If we're not confident and we don't believe, we can't swing. It's a cause and effect relationship. If the guy who is trying to break five boards hesitates, he's going to break his knuckles. A warrior doesn't try to defeat the dragon; he slays it. No matter what, a warrior has unflinching confidence that obliterates doubt and destroys hesitation. No matter your physical skill level, all of you can develop this mindset if you work at it.

Game Mode is about being serious; it's about attitude. It's about leaving your real life in the parking lot and stepping into a competitive frame of mind. It's about developing the mental perspective that transforms passive puppies into aggressive dogs. It's about developing a second set of skills, the mental skills of a competitor. It's about being able to step-up with confidence, and compete.

S U M M A R Y

- Don't hide from the truth.

- Where you fit on the Dog Scale is up to you.

- Welcome doubt and fear.

- Use the Meltdown Meter to check your composure.

- Don't be a jumper, talk yourself down.

- Raise your confidence with BIG-Dog Vision.

- Executing under pressure takes guts. Guts are about attitude.

"Remember doubt is inevitable, but choking is preventable. When we truthfully look at how we react emotionally in competition, and then master the techniques for controlling our Dogs, we're able to step-up and compete, with confidence."   — Steve Knight

Chapter Five

BIG-Dog Vision • Believe

If there's one chapter I encourage you to read over and over until you understand and master what is presented, it's this one.

Get real, create a vision and believe. Controlling mind and emotions is the battle that decides a champion.

As I watch athletes train and prepare for state and national level competition, there's one thing that perplexes me: After repeated failure the majority haven't realized that harnessing their mental power is just as, or even more important than, developing their physical skills or improving conditioning.

Think of it this way: Why labor over technique and grind through conditioning if you don't believe? Why practice your brains out if you can't control the intense emotion that comes with state and national level competition?

Personally, the reason I competed was to win the title tournaments. In order to accomplish that, my emotions had to be my friend—not my enemy.

"Courage is not the absence of fear, but the ability to carry on in spite of it."

— Mark Twain

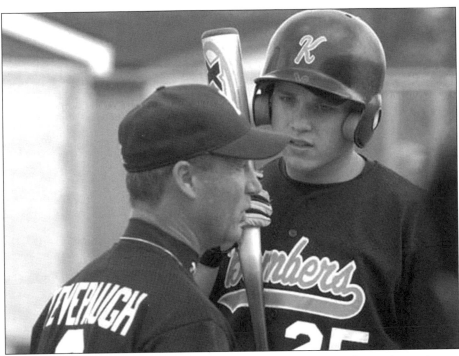

Above: Chagrin Falls, OH: Kenston High School Head Baseball Coach Randy Tevepaugh discusses hitting strategy with centerfielder Andy Harsh. Harsh went on to get the game winning hit to send the Bombers to the district semi-finals. Photo by Kenston Baseball.

Left Page: Jackson, Tennessee: Union University Bulldog's freshman (2003) Steven Sweat, third baseman and pitcher, steps up to the plate at the TranSouth Conference Baseball Tournament. Photo by Lindsay Stavish.

Unique Approach

Typically, visualization is thought of as seeing victory—imagining yourself blasting the winning homer or envisioning the team dog-pile after making the clutch defensive play to end the game that won the championship.

Another common technique to offset doubt and intimidation is positive self-talk – mentally repeating positive statements attempting to convince yourself you're not really scared. I never had much success with either of those methods because they didn't get at the root of the issue: No matter how experienced we are, in pressure situations we're going to get scared and emotions have to be managed.

With help from my first coach, and through much trial and error over years of competing, I developed what I call BIG-Dog Vision—a unique approach to visualization that replaces doubt and intimidation with genuine confidence.

Two Minds

As I explained in the previous chapter, we all have two minds—our little dog and our BIG-Dog. Both minds have different sets of detrimental emotions that have to be understood and managed to be successful in pressure situations. Our little dog mind

"I guarantee this; you'll never find 'the zone' with your little dog at the helm—worried, shaking, and doubtful."

is always doubtful and never thinks it can accomplish anything. On the other hand, our BIG-Dog mind is usually over confident and often focuses on the wrong things. To be a successful competitor (not just a baseball player, but a confident, clutch player) it's a necessity to understand your two minds to effectively manage your emotions in pressure situations.

Rough Territory

BIG-Dog Vision techniques put us in touch with our competitive minds—both of them—and for a lot of us this is rough territory. Looking at ourselves truthfully is not something very many of us want to do. But, if we want to be successful competitors, not just athletes, we have no choice. To have control over our emotions we have to know where they come from, which is why envisioning victory or chanting positive statements is not very effective. Those techniques don't help us deal with the core issue, which is doubt will always be part of competing, and that ignoring those emotions or trying to talk them away is an illusion and won't help the process of building high-level competitive confidence.

Learning BIG-Dog Vision isn't hard if we're willing to look beyond the image we project and be truthful with ourselves.

Did I lose you there? The majority of us walk around looking all confident and powerful, but, actuality that's only a projection of an image we've mentally created. A lot of us are trying to trick ourselves into believing we're BIG-Dogs, but as soon as a real challenge presents itself we crash—because our confidence is founded on fantasy and we can't take fantasy into battle.

The sooner we look ourselves square in the competitive face and see who really comes out when we go into battle—our little dog or our BIG-Dog—the sooner we're able to manage how our minds work. This is how little dogs find their BIG-Dog, and how BIG-Dogs calm themselves down.

First, we have to be truthful about being who we really are and how we mentally react in competition. If we're little dogs, we need to admit that so we can motivate ourselves to find our BIG-Dog.

Understanding our true competitive confidence is what BIG-Dog Vision is all about. It helps mere athletes transform into confident, successful competitors. But, for some of us, this is a difficult journey because we don't want to face who we truly are in a competitive environment.

Many athletes limit their training to one element, the physical, because it's the easiest to understand. But, to be successful competitors, we need to consistently work on two elements—the body AND the mind.

Hard Work

A general perspective in the athletic community, especially at the kids and high school level, is that HARD WORK is the cure-all for everything. Respectfully, I disagree.

I've known many athletes who worked as hard as anyone, on and off the field, but go to tournaments and fall apart. If hard work were the only ticket necessary to win gold, many more non-champions would be champions.

It's a misconception that hard physical work translates into mental dominance. What has happened is the lines have gotten blurred.

Yes, acknowledged, athletes have to develop a work ethic that many people will not commit to. Athletes have to work hard and sacrifice, and yes, there is a certain mental element that goes along with building commitment, work tolerance, and oxygen exchange capability (conditioning). But that isn't the mental side of competing, that's the mental side of not being a physical wimp.

In weightlifting, doing rep after rep, set after set, day after day is a "mental thing," but that's not competitive dominance. That's training hard. Competing is an entirely different planet, totally unlike training or practice.

The majority of young athletes could train until they're blue in the face, but as they walk onto the battlefield would still lay-an-egg because they haven't learned how to control their fears or focus their minds.

Coaches: If you drill your player's minds along with their bodies, it will immediately elevate your team's competitive intensity. They will be able to compete at a higher level almost instantly.

When training, it's much easier to focus on the body because we can see it. It's easy to see the body sweat, it's easy to see a great swing and it's easy to see a well-executed play. In contrast, it's much harder to see someone's mind working, or not working. But, if we're trained in "seeing" mental confidence, it's as easy as evaluating a solid cut, a great glove, or a crisp throw.

The bigger issue is we can't lie about making contact – we either did or we didn't. The mind is hidden. Plus, most of us have a tendency to lie about our emotions and confidence because we think we'll be perceived as weak, which is a little dog tendency.

The first step in finding your player deep inside is being truthful with yourself.

Physical Toughness

Physical toughness – the will to train hard, and play banged-up, broken and fatigued – is a part of mental toughness, but overcoming physical pain has little to do with competitive confidence. The physical punishment requirement to practice like a madman is why so many kids bail, but enduring physical difficulties alone does not create mental competitive dominance.

Don't misunderstand. I'm not saying that monster hard work is not a vital ingredient to being a successful player, it definitely is. But that's only half of the equation. We also need the mental skills of a competitor to walk out of state or nationals a champion.

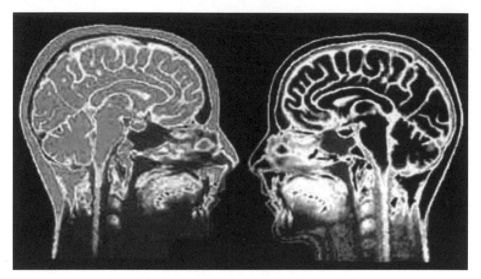

Represented is one of the key concepts from the book: One mind, two dogs. With opposing mindsets-one scared to death (left) and the other focused and confident—our little dog and our BIG-Dog continuously face-off trying to dominate our thinking, which directly impacts our ability to perform. That seesaw battle is fought from second to second, and only you can decide which of your Dogs controls your actions. Source: Not available.

At state and nationals all of the top ranked players have worked hard … physically. It's the athletes who work hard mentally as well who take home gold.

Mental Toughness

Mental toughness is being able to deal with the rigors of self-evaluation – the internal psychology of how one views oneself. Not feels—VIEWS. And there is a BIG difference. One is opinion, the other reality.

Mental evaluation is far scarier territory than physical evaluation, especially in the 21st Century. Why? Because a low percentage of our society hold themselves accountable, apprenticeship does not exist, and everyone thinks they're entitled. Few people want to work for greatness. To openly look at ourselves with any level of realism is like pulling teeth. We run and hide.

Make sense? Most of us, not just teens, do not want to see ourselves for who we really are inside. But as athletes, to be able to control our emotions we have to know our minds and how our minds work.

Mental dominance is being able to see our fears and doubt and then overcome them. It's a process that has to be practiced before it can be mastered.

As a world-class competitor it's my experience that truth with oneself is where the power lies. When we get out of our own way, and channel the tremendous mental power that we all have, allowing our personality, physical skills, and hard work to take over, it's an incredible experience that we never forget. This is often referred to as "the zone." It almost feels effortless, and to achieve it takes a combination of physical and mental skills. We all have the capability; we just have to work at it, to realize it.

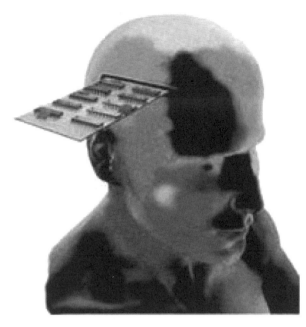

Another key concept from the book:Our competitive psychology is programmable. As humans, we can transform our dominant psychology—natural tendencies—from doubtful to confident by reprogramming our competitive minds. By using BIG-Dog Vision techniques we lessen little dog tendencies and increase BIG-Dog dominance. Image source: Not available.

I guarantee this; you will never find the zone with your little dog in control—worried, shaking and doubtful.

Mental-Evaluation

First, lets create a comparison to get a clear picture. We could easily do a physical evaluation, correct? I could travel to any team in the county and hand out a physical evaluation sheet for each player that had a 1– 3 rating in three categories – technique, endurance, and power. And if everyone gave their truthful opinion and the evaluations were averaged, it would provide a pretty accurate picture of each player's physical capability. Right? No big deal. As athletes, we're sizing each other up constantly. We know who is getting stronger, who's looking leaner, who's getting quicker, and who's acting like a wimp. Those variables change from week to week. We keep up-to-date mental data on our group's physical capability. It's just what we athletes do.

What about confidence and heart? Actually, I think we do the same thing, maybe a little less consciously. But, we know who is confident and who is timid, who will crack under pressure and who won't, who is aggressive and who is passive, and to what degree. Just like the physical variables, those confidence and heart variables change from minute to minute, day-to-day and week-to-week.

For example, if I asked everyone on a team who was the strongest, instantly I'd hear a name. If I asked who had the best technique, I might hear a couple of names. But, if

"Don't just look for mistakes you made physically, look and identify your psychology: were you scared, tentative, or confident?"

I asked who was the toughest, it would get quiet. Even though we know who the toughest is, that's not something we're going to quickly acknowledge. If I asked who mentally had the most confidence, same thing—quiet. But, if I asked who choked the most, BAM! Names would come out. We can nail those guys.

Do you see the parallels I am drawing? Guys, it's more important to know the strengths of your mind than of your body. I'll take a mental giant over a physical powerhouse any day. Once you pop a hole in the powerhouse's illusion of his physical superiority, he's done. He'll crash and burn. That's the main thing little dogs don't realize about attitude – it's all in our minds. We create attitude. You know the saying, "The bigger they are the harder they fall." Where do you think that comes from?

Mental evaluation is harder than physical evaluation. This is because our minds work like blenders. When we add emotion it's like pushing the puree button—the lid flies off and excuses splatter everywhere.

Take emotion out of the formula. It's like taking taste out of fueling—it doesn't belong. Emotion and clear, unbiased mental-evaluation are like oil and water, they do not go together.

It's much easier for coaches to do a physical evaluation of their teams than a psychological evaluation. Here is a general way to evaluate a team. Physical: technique, endurance, and power. Mental: confidence and heart. Use a 1-3 rating in each category and after compiling each individual player's rating, you would have a team rating.

If a team's confidence and heart rating didn't average at least a 2.7, mental practice should be long and hard until they get there. Then, when the team walks into any stadium in the country it blazes with confidence instead of projecting arrogance. I've seen this positive transformation take place within individuals many times and a baseball team is no more than a group of individuals.

Mental-evaluation is similar to any touchy subject—once we bring it out in the open, it's not as touchy as we think. Evaluating confidence and heart is the same thing. Once we bring it out into the open and don't run away from it, we can start to work on it, which is how we improve.

Projecting

We all project. That's how we get our personalities out of ourselves and into the environment. We manipulate the projection to get what we want in a specific environment. If you think about it, you know exactly what I'm talking about.

The attitude and personality you project when you're sitting at the dinner table with your family is way different than the attitude you project when you're hanging with your buddies.

Player unknown. Photo by Teri James.

We control those different outward projections, whether we realize it or not. We learn how to do this very early in life, and, as our personalities grow, our projections multiply and change.

One of the mistakes BIG-Dogs make at competitions is they are constantly projecting, which takes a tremendous amount of energy.

On a day-to-day basis BIG-Dogs project their physical superiority and aggressive tendencies within their social groups. This is how they establish their "alphadom."

BIG-Dog Vision ™
Believe

During pressure situations, when your team needs you most, visualizing success or chanting positive statements will not prevent choking.

Use **BIG-Dog Vision** to replace feelings of doubt with genuine confidence, so you can deliver the level of play you dream of: Clutch game winning play.

Let your BIG-Dog out!

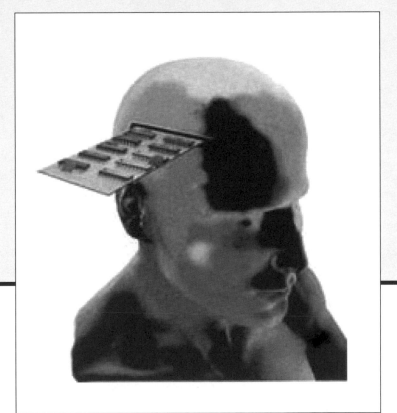

Artist Unknown

"You gotta believe."

— Tug McGraw

But at a competition it's a total waste of energy, and worse, it's distracting.

Staring down or mugging opposing players, projecting the tractor-beam stare across the field is a total waste. It's a little dog trying to act like a BIG-Dog. You're diverting valuable energy and concentration into the outer environment. You're actually putting on a display rather then preparing to hit one out of the park.

Weightlifters can be the worst at this – yelling, slapping, huffing and puffing. What do they think they're doing, intimidating the weights? I don't think so. Or some might say, "That's what gets me up." I don't think so. Bottom line, it's an outward display of fear. They're scared to death and they don't know how to channel their emotions, so they let them out all over the arena, which is rookie behavior and a tremendous energy drain.

As a competitor I used to enjoy watching all of those goofballs doing their displays of fear, because I knew they were exhausting themselves, which gave me a competitive advantage.

Don't project—at all. It's worthless. Harness and focus your emotional energy. Dominating is not about acting; it's about doing.

Harness & Control

To me the word "harness" means we already have it. We don't have to get it or develop it. We all have incredible mental power that must be harnessed and controlled or it's our undoing.

The reason I can say that with such conviction is we're all equipped with the ability to fight with extreme intensity, if necessary. It's a basic survival capability. Just because some of us choose to shrivel-up and mentally submit when we're scared doesn't mean that we don't have incredible mental intensity. It just means we choose not to use it. That is a HUGE distinction.

Harnessing and controlling emotions is the key to a player's competitive success—or his destruction. The main point is: You have it, it's your choice whether you use it or not.

Open Minds

"Minds are like parachutes, they only work when they're open."
(Sir James Dewar, Scientist)

I encourage all you Dogs to open your minds and be truthful with yourselves. A great discovery lies ahead—seeing your true competitive mindset. And once grappled with and mastered, you'll have BIG-Dog Vision on command.

All you BIG-Dogs realize you already have it, so get out of your own way, show some teeth and focus your Dog.

All you little dogs realize you already have it, so believe in yourself, show some teeth, and let your BIG-Dog out.

Joliet, Illinois: Joliet Catholic Academy's Ryan Lincoln-#19, protects first base during a game against Naperville Central at Sliver Cross Field. Photographer and base runner unknown.

Left: Winchester, Virginia: Collegiate summer league Winchester Royal's Nelson Gord gets caught in a rundown between players from the Covington, Lumberjacks. Photo by Jeff Taylor/Winchester Star.

Right: Plano, Texas: Plano West High School's Taylor Wyrick stays alert ready to make the play. Photo source: Mark Bromberg.

The Process

Now we get to the nuts and bolts of looking truthfully at our performance, our two Dogs, and how they really are.

Again, this is rough territory guys. For a lot of us it's when all sorts of mental blocks go up and excuses start erupting. That's natural. We live in a defensive society. But let me tell you, every champion has to go though this personal evaluation in order to genuinely be confident in battle. As competitors, we have to know ourselves in order to control ourselves.

Hopefully, you have video of past performances. We're going to focus on two totally opposite outcomes. The first tape should be of a performance when you were a BIG-Dog; when you were confident, executed well and felt like a champion. The other is when you were a little dog—when you were scared, intimidated, and choked.

How did you just react internally to even thinking about watching the choked video? Did you get a lump in your throat? Did you get a little nervous? Feel a little weird? You probably don't even want to go there. Well guess what, get over it and take a look.

Now, sit down with someone you trust and respect, who can talk with you about how and why you felt the way you did. For you young guys, it should be someone older, with some competitive experience. First, review Tape #2. What is your internal reaction? How do you handle watching yourself choking? Are you embarrassed? Are you hiding emotionally? Making excuses? Or are you being truthful and learning

Get Real
Look At Yourself Truthfully

The image below is the most important image in this book—our opposing competitive minds:

(Left) Our little dog: cloudy, foggy, and confused—our doubting psychology. **"I can't."**

(Right) Our BIG-Dog: clear, crisp, and focused—our confident psychology. **"I can."**

Get Real! Look at your competitive minds truthfully. Know with clarity whether you're doubtful, tentative, or confident.

Grappling with your *true competitive* psychology is how to build the mental skills of a confident Player. Beware, the first step is the most difficult: Get Real.

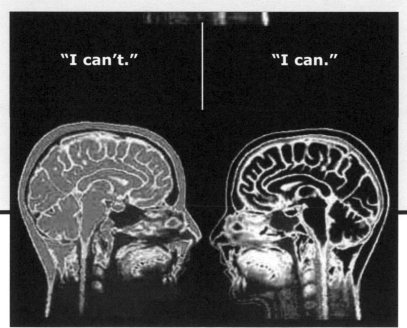

"I can't."   "I can."

Artist Unknown

"Whether you think you can or you can't you're probably right."
— Henry Ford

something? Does watching that real experience shrink you or motivate you? Take a serious look at your little dog in action. Don't look for flawed techniques or how the pitcher blew that fastball by you, look at your little dog factor, your lack of confidence and execution. Ask yourself questions: Why were you so shook? There are reasons. We don't have a meltdown just because. Have a meaningful discussion with your trusted friend, and get to the bottom of why you choked. Then, review Tape #1, when you dominated—when your BIG-Dog came out to play. Analyze your BIG-Dog factor with the same questions. Why were you confident? Break the reasons down. "I don't know" is mentally lazy and lame. Get to the bottom of why you felt confident. Be able to explain yourself why in both performances, so you can clearly understand.

Trust me here. Getting real with ourselves is the first step to improving. Again, don't look for mistakes you made physically, look and identify your psychology. Why were you scared or confident, and to what degree?

Are you starting to see how this works? It's really simple if we're willing to be real with ourselves. Once we go through the process a few (hundred) times, we start to see a pattern develop: scared, tentative, or confident. Each, of course, has degrees, but we find ourselves in one of those three categories the majority of the time.

First baseman: There are many occasions at first base when you have to make a great dig to get the out. Sometimes this can go unnoticed as opposed to the dramatic diving play your team- mate made to get the ball in the hole and fire it to you in time. But when you miss one of those bad throws, all the negative attention focuses on you. Many if not all of you at first base have experienced this. Try to find one of those missed digs on tape and watch yourself closely, specif- ically focusing on your mental state. Where was your competitive mind? Were you doubtful? Scared? Were you lackadaisical and unfocused with your effort? Being in the right frame of mind greatly increases your chances of making the tough play. Be real with yourself so you can identify your mindset, which will help you learn to focus during BIG-Play opportunities.

BIG-Dog Vision DVDs

Now it's time to create some mental BIG-Dog Vision DVDs. One for each of our emotional categories: scared, tentative, and confident.

No doubt you guys are starting to see how this works, but I will walk you though the process anyhow. Remember, if you're not completely truthful with yourself, none of this will work.

Scared DVD: Just like the process I just described for evaluating the videos of per- vious little dog performances, mentally go back to one or two more game situations when you were scared out of your mind, when you could not even think. Now this is the important part. Clearly document what sent you into little dog mode. Was it the pitcher's reputation? He beat you in the past? He struck out the best hitter on your team? Or was it a big game? See yourself at the game, and mentally rewind the experience. Document very clearly what happened from the first thought that tweaked you, because when you mentally rewind and look, you're getting a real-time view of one of your competitive minds—your scared little dog. Once you've remembered a couple of experiences, and have analyzed the reasons why you were scared, burn those experiences and feelings on your Scared DVD.

Tentative DVD: This is very similar to the Scared DVD, but not as intense. Probably, you'll be tentative more often in game situations than you will be truly scared. Go back to a couple of games when you were tentative, when you hesitated, and clearly document why? Why were you feeling uncertain? Give yourself specific, real reasons. Don't guess—know. Because what you're replaying in your mind is not a fantasy, it's a real experience of your tentative little dog. Once you've remembered a couple of game experiences and have analyzed the reasons why you were tentative, mentally burn those experiences and feelings on your Tentative DVD.

Confident DVD: This is the fun DVD. Make sure you have several confident game experiences recorded. Use the same process as above. Ask yourself questions and understand why you were confident. Be very clear about which experiences you burn to your confident DVD. You will use this DVD over and over and over. Why? Because the confident DVD is the one you will insert in your head when you're tentative or scared.

It is vital that you understand the full spectrum of competitive emotions: scared, tentative and confident.

Insert Disk

The photo on page 58 is probably the most important photo is this book. Those are our two minds: our little dog and our BIG-Dog—our scared psychology and our confident psychology. And those two opposite emotions are constantly battling for control.

Now review the picture on page 59. That's how we have to think when we're scared or tentative, we're reprogramming our competitive minds. We're replacing doubt with confidence by understanding why we're going into a meltdown, telling our little dog where to go and focusing on real experiences when we were BIG-Dogs.

Are you starting to make the connection? When we're truthful with ourselves we can see our competitive minds work—both of them—then with BIG-Dog Vision we can edit or dismiss our weaknesses and confirm our confidence, which translates into mental dominance. Mentally reprogramming ourselves is as simple as inserting a disk, but in order for the reprogramming to work, we have to be truthful, so we can believe.

The next step is early meltdown detection. To know when our little dog is taking over, before he has us sniveling in the corner. Learn how to detect where you're at on the Meltdown Meter, and how to bring yourself back down once you climb above a 2.0. Coach yourself up and reason with yourself. Ask yourself why your stomach is in knots, and why you don't believe in yourself? See your BIG-Dog come out and chase

Create a mental screening room with as much detail as possible, so you can escape and reprogram anytime, anywhere. Image source: Not available.

your little dog into submission. Create visions that will help you see WHY you can believe in yourself—because you can. Eventually, with practice, we learn how to detect and control our little dog psychology. Remember, it's all about attitude and attitude is entirely in our minds.

The entire point of this process is to vividly see yourself emotionally crashing, and then purposefully taking a clear look at why you're doubtful. Then, you can figure out how to recover, and then execute.

No matter what happens, no matter what stadium you're in, no matter whom you're up against, you have a similar experience on either your scared or tentative DVD. That's why you have those DVDs—so you can relate to having been there before. Now you insert your confident DVD to bring yourself back to reality. You're a stud … believe in yourself.

I mentioned in Chapter 1, visualization wasn't about the rewards; it's about the battle. And even though I'm pretty certain now you understand why, let me clarify: visualizing rewards is OK—if it's at the end of a session. If you want to create your DVDs so that once you control your little dog, and your BIG-Dog comes out and dominates, and then you see yourself ripping the game winning homer, and the crowd erupts, and you're holding the championship trophy with your team, getting the girl and going to the victory dinner … that's all good.

Screening Room

In order to utilize BIG-Dog Vision anytime, anywhere, creating a mental screening room can be helpful. Review the picture on page 69. Now that's a screening room.

Take the time to create your personal screening room (mentally) in detail, the greater details the more real it becomes.

To share—my personal screening room is worth about $100,000.00 (Hey, this is my creation, and it's monopoly money, so who cares). Everything is the latest digital equipment: 52″ flat screen, DVD player, and monster surround sound with mega bass. The songs I play as I approach the battlefield rock, sort of like the scene in the helicopter at the beginning of <u>Predator</u>, when they're getting ready to be dropped into the combat zone (Side note: That moment in a tournament, when the energy is flying and it's moments away from performance time is the most fun. Man, I get worked up just writing about competing). I also have some frills in my screening room: three plush black recliners, a refrigerator, Play Station 2, and an Xbox. You name it, and my screening room has it.

Sometimes (mentally) I invite friends over to review performance DVDs with me, when I need input, but my recliner is in the middle, and I have the controls. Are you seeing where I'm going with this? It's not only a place to review your performance and control your Dogs; your personal screening room is a safe, comfortable place that you can mentally escape to anytime, no matter where you are. It's a tremendous tension reliever in pressure situations. You don't have to just review mental DVDs of your performance—you can put in whatever DVD you like.

Take the time to create your imaginary screening room with as much detail as possible, the more detail the more real it will be.

Patience

Patience, players. Developing BIG-Dog Vision is a process that takes time and practice. It's just like developing physical skills that you had to practice over and over until you got it right—until the skill felt natural, and eventually you could use it at will. BIG-Dog Vision is the same thing.

Give yourself time and be diligent about practicing visualization. In no time you'll know how to subdue your little dog and control your emotions. BIG-Dog Vision is what will help you transform doubt into confidence, so you can deliver the level of play you're capable of—clutch, game winning play.

"There is no elevator to success.
You have to take the stairs."

— Mike Espy

S U M M A R Y

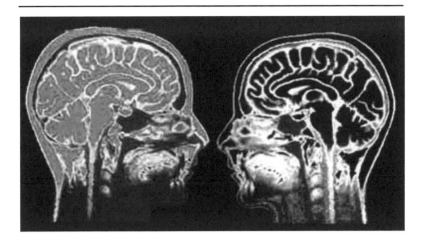

- ◆ Get real.

- ◆ Look your true competitive psychology square in the face; are you scared, tentative, or confident?

- ◆ Create a mental screening room to reprogram your minds anytime, anywhere.

- ◆ Watch your confident DVDs to calm little dog fears and knock self-doubt out of the park.

- ◆ Don't project. It's worthless.

- ◆ Be patient. BIG-Dog Vision takes practice.

- ◆ Yes, you can transform into a confident competitor.

"Get real. Be patient. Look your competitive core dead in the eyes. Give yourself time to understand your doubts; and be persistent about building your confident DVD collection. If you're truthful, in no time you'll have a better grasp of your competitive emotions, and how to manage them." — Steve Knight

Chapter Six

THE BATTLE • Composure

Now it's time to play some ball. All the preparation is behind you. You're just chilling in the stands. Waiting. You feel confident, but uncertain. You don't know how sharp you'll be until you step on to the field or into the batter's box. Now the real battle begins – the confidence battle – the battle over composure.

Transitions

The battle over composure is fought in the transitions. As we move mentally and physically from our casual everyday life to our intensely focused competitive life, we go through a transition. From home to the ballpark, from watching TV on the couch to the batter's box ripping one down the line. There are short transitions and long transitions, easy transitions and hard transitions. If this example seems too drastic, that

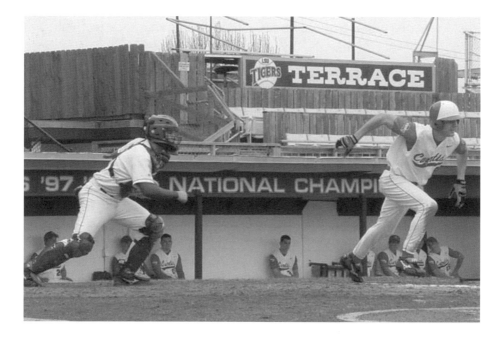

"What the mind and imagination believe, the human body can achieve."

— Author Unknown

Above: Sacramento, Ca: Sheldon High School shortstop fires a throw to first. Head Coach Chris Terry. Photo source: Elk Grove Citizen.

Left Page: Baton Rouge, LA: Photo from the Kiwanis Baseball Invitational. A player from multiple state champions John Curtis High School sprints to first. Photo source Rick Martin.

casual and competitive are two different worlds—perfect—they are. The transition from an affectionate family member to an intensely competitive player is that drastic.

As you pull into the parking lot at an away game, get off the bus and take the field, you're going through a transition. Once you settle down after the first inning, you go through a series of transitions. It's a constant roller coaster: focus, then chill—focus, then chill. Each cycle has a transition.

The majority of time the transition is where our little dogs take over. It's when we talk ourselves out of what we can do, and into what we can't do. The transition is when most of us go nuts, meltdown emotionally, and lose our composure.

Example: The time between being up fifth as the inning begins to on-deck ten minutes later is when we either savor the competitive moment and get pumped about the executing, or crash under the "what if" pressure and miss BIG-Play opportunities.

"The discipline required at a major tournament is probably the hardest discipline is, especially for teens."

Without a consciousness of transitions, how can we go from being mentally relaxed to competitively focused? We can't. In order to move from one place to another, either physically or mentally, there has to be a transition. Mentally it's a weird emotional zone, a place where expectations meet convictions. Going through the transition is when we need the mental skills of a seasoned competitor.

During those minutes, hours, or days before intense competitions, much of our mental/emotional time is spent in that mid-land between casual and competitive – battling self-doubt and "what if" possibilities—which is a natural, continuous, before every game process. But once we get close to the actual competition, not just thinking about it, that's the center of the transition when our BIG-Dog competitive skills are needed most.

Patience & Focus

One of the keys to successfully maintaining composure is realizing that games are a hurry-up and wait situation. Waiting starts as soon as you get to the ballpark and there's a lot more waiting—inaction—during games. Defensively, depending on your position, there can be huge amounts of time when nothing comes your way, but you have to stay mentally alert, ready to react. Offensively, even if you're a starter, there's a lot of downtime between at-bats. Those downtimes are when we mentally wander and lose our competitive edge. The downtimes are when patience and focus are critical to maintaining a competitive mindset.

The underlying theme for successful games and tournaments are patience, focus and composure.

Discipline is what brings those three elements together. The discipline required at major, multi-day tournaments is probably the hardest discipline there is – especially for teens. Not only do you guys want to run around all night getting into mischief (chasing cheerleaders), you also want to plot and explore all day long.

Here goes the dad/coach stern-faced finger-pointing speech: get a grip. Why are you there? Why have you worked so hard? Is it party time or game time? Why end up performing poorly because you indulged your pleasure interests? Why not battle like a focused BIG-Dog all the way to the last out of the championship round? Well? Make positive decisions that propel you toward your dream.

Sticking with straight talk: stay focused. Don't blow it once you get to state or an important title tournament. Plotting and indulging social activities will alter your focus and lower your competitive intensity. Like it or not, winning state isn't supposed to be a full-on, girl chasing social adventure. Winning a multi-game state tournament takes an extraordinary level of concentration and conviction. The reality is: you can't have it all.

Chagrin Falls, OH: Kenston's High School's All-Ohio catcher, Josh Schmidt tags out a Stow H.S. base runner in high school baseball action. Head Coach Randy Tevepaugh. Photo by Kenston Baseball.

For all of you scammers who are smiling and thinking that you can have it all – that you can party, chase girls, and still perform at a superior level – sorry, you're in fantasyland.

This point is so important and for many of you traveling with your team is a new experience, so let's go over it one more time. I've seen the distractions at state and nationals derail many would be champions because they lost their competitive focus and decided (unconsciously) to indulge themselves socially. I encourage you to keep your head on straight and conserve your energy for the game. In other words, when you're off the field, don't deviate from your Game Mode mindset. If your focus wanders before the last out, the likelihood is you'll suffer some sort of negative consequences.

This isn't a karma thing; it's a focus thing. The mind can only do one thing at a time. Switching from casual mode to Game Mode isn't easy for most of us. And even though we have to put our laser-beam focus on pause a lot of the time, we must keep one foot in the mission knowing that BIG-Play moments are minutes away. Mentally wandering or fully engaging social activities is a big mistake during competitions.

Trust me, state is not the place to goof around. The mind and habits of a BIG-Dog competitor are focused, confident, and determined. Try not to fall into the little dog trap of mistaking your state tournament for Disneyland or some sort of group vacation. Get a grip guys. At games and tournaments, especially the title tournaments, you need to be the most focused and the most disciplined. Yeah, have fun, but don't forget why you're there—you are there to compete.

Timing

As soon as the Ump yells, "Play ball," the game is on and the emotional roller coaster lurches forward. Your mind races and your stomach twists. The mental "what if" battle goes into full gear, especially if it's a big game and there are high expectations for you to perform.

The type of timing we're discussing here is not about a swing, a windup, or a throw; it's about the flow of the game and mentally transitioning from relaxed to focused.

As we've discussed previously, staying intensely focused all of the time is almost impossible, so paying attention to the flow of the game and how you fit into that flow is vital to being confident when BIG-Play opportunities present themselves. In other words, knowing when to turn your laser-beam focus off is just as important as knowing when to turn it on.

Offensively, if there are several batters until your up, disengage the game for a few minutes to give your mind and emotions a rest. Defensively, if there's a break in the flow to the plate, for whatever reason: changing pitchers, coaches arguing with umpires, etc., turn the laser-beam focus off for a minute to conserve energy and to rest your most powerful weapon—your mind.

The bottom line regarding timing is to learn how to stay connected with the flow of the game to better manage the 20 or 30 times you'll transition from relaxed to focused in each game.

Peoria Chiefs players sit dejected in the dugout trailing Lansing 10-3 as the ninth inning begins. Their mood would lighten considerably later in the inning when they rallied with eight runs to win the Midwest League championship in Lansing. Photo and caption by Chris Curry/Journal Star.

Second basemen: Disengaging is twice as important for you, especially with everything you must pay attention to defensively. You have to know who is covering second on a steal, be aware of a bunt situation to cover first, act as the cutoff man, and field your position. Knowing where to go and when to go there is vital, which means your laser-beam focus needs to be dialed-in every time you are on the field. But this can be mentally draining, as I'm sure many of you have experienced. Late in the game is the wrong time to goof up and not be at second when the pitchers whips around to pick off the runner. Learn when to disengage at the proper times for a brief mental rest; so late in the game when it's on the line your laser-beam concentration is working to its full capacity.

Dugout Dynamics

Wow! The dugout. It can either be your best friend or your worst enemy. Intense coaches, freaked out teammates, and too much time to focus on the wrong things. Learning how to deal with the dynamics of the dugout is far more critical than the dynamics on the field, unless you're the pitcher or the catcher.

A successful defense, of course, is vital to winning games. But again, unless you're the pitcher or the catcher, plays happen so fast you don't have a lot of time to talk yourself out of being a stud. The dugout, however, is a different story.

Step-Up
It's About Proving Yourself

Uncertainty, adversity, injury, intimidation; it doesn't matter, a BIG-Dog looks difficulty square in the face and overcomes.

In other words, it ain't gonna be easy. Step-Up.

Everyday, all season long, in every game, one way or another, it comes down to proving yourself: are you a little dog or a BIG-Dog?

Decide—then live with it.

Cowboy unknown. Photo by David Huber.

"Show me a guy who's afraid to look bad and I'll show you a guy you can beat every time."

— Lou Brock

"I've seen the distractions at state derail many would be gold medallists, because they lost their competitive focus."

The transitions in the dugout are when most of you emotionally crash. As the line-up progresses toward your spot, especially in pressure situations, your confidence routines are needed most. The specifics of your routines are different for each of you.

Personally, I'm the type that needs to disconnect from everyone around me because I'm easily distracted. It's not that I don't like or want to support my teammates; it's because transitions take me a little longer. Other competitors can flip the switch and go from casual mode to Game Mode in an instant. My process is not so quick and requires a little more concentration.

All of our styles for getting focused are different. Some of us can handle more distractions than others. Example: Some people can read effectively in a crowed, noisy room. For me that's impossible.

Chatty teammates, or teammates who are melting down, emotionally throwing up all over the place (figuratively speaking) are the worst; it drives me nuts—doubt can be contagious. My simple technique to keep other's doubt eruptions off me and to narrow my focus is to put on headphones with some rockin music and throw a towel over my head for a few minutes before I'm up to center myself. For those of you who find talking relaxing, make sure you hook up with teammates who have a similar competitive style.

Some of you need to get angry and pace around in order to pump yourself up. There a many ways to get the promised land of self-confidence and all of those different competitive styles are the reasons why I call it "dugout dynamics." There is a lot going on and everyone is in close proximity to each other. You can't escape your teammates' energies, so it's very important to figure out what works best for you and then to make sure you put yourself in the position to make it happen. In other words, don't let the dynamics of the dugout take you out of your competitive mindset. Take control and do whatever you need to do to stay focused and confident.

On-Deck

On-Deck is where confidence truly starts to get tested—"actual" confidence, not fantasy confidence. Sensing where you are at on the Meltdown Meter is vital as you wait for your turn at the plate. If you're less then a 1.0 you better get a little more respectful. If you're quickly climbing above a 3.0, tweaked, mentally escape to your screening room, plug in your BIG-Dog confident DVD, focus on your strengths, calm your doubts and breathe. Did I mention breathe? I mean breathe. Oxygen will help you manage the adrenaline that is dumping into your blood stream from the excitement of pre-competition.

Plano, Texas: Plano West Wolves base runner attempts to beat the tag from an Allen High School infielder. Plano West Head Coach: Blake Boydston. Photo source: Mark Bromberg.

Let's pause a moment to talk about adrenaline. Powerful stuff. Without getting technical, adrenaline's bottom-line is RUN!!! When we start to feel threatened, glands dump adrenaline into our blood stream, which quickly increases our physical and mental capability. On-Deck is usually when the first adrenaline dump happens.

There are a couple of significant adrenaline rush side affects that you need to be aware of. The first and worst is when too much adrenaline is dumped at once, which is usually caused by genuine doubt or extreme fear—your little dog is freaking. A monster adrenaline rush can make you feel nauseous (yep, some puke), lightheaded, unfocused, physically weak, and all sorts of other negative side effects. The downside of an adrenaline rush can leave you feeling lethargic and tired – sort of a let down.

Stanford Cardinals catcher Donny Lucy shows great swing mechanics as he makes solid contact. Photo by David Gonzales (www.gonzalesphoto.com).

The way out of a monster adrenaline rush is oxygen and concentration; breathe and talk yourself down. Control it; don't let it control you. There is more adrenaline where that came from, which is a good thing, so don't freak-out. Compose yourself emotionally and get back in control. When it's finally your turn at the plate you'll be focused and ready to compete.

Most world-class athletes have learned how to control adrenaline rushes, but it takes many years of high-level competition to really master adrenaline. At the very least, know that an adrenaline rush feels edgy, nervous and weird. Breathe; it's a good thing.

Back to On-Deck.

Every at-bat is important, but some are clutch: when your team needs you most. Those are the times at the plate when you prove whether you're just a player or a clutch competitor, and on-deck is where the main transition from casual to competitive takes place. On-deck is when many players let their mind emotionally wander and they get lost in "what if" possibilities, which is mental chatter that is typically negative and totally unproductive.

Example: As you're warming up, studying the pitcher's rhythm as your teammate tries to execute coach's instructions, you're either focused and confident or mentally scattered thinking about negative outcomes. What if I strike out; what if I fly out; what if I hit into a double play? Then, with those thoughts at the center of your mind, you see all sorts of undesirable social consequences: you let your team down, you don't get the scholarship, and life ends as you know it. Those, and many other variations are negative "what if" possibilities.

Now that you have a better understanding of your two minds, I bet you know which one of your dogs is doing the negative "what if" thinking. Exactly: your little dog. Your BIG-Dog isn't interested in the negative; if your BIG-Dog engages in "what if" thinking it's going to be positive; seeing yourself cracking one out of the park, winning the game, getting the scholarship and your team holding the championship trophy.

On-deck is when you employ the mental skills you've been working on to calm your little dog down so your BIG-Dog can come out and play.

The Pitch

Stepping into the batter's box in any situation, let alone during a clutch opportunity, is clearly an emotional challenge. If you were strapped up with a heart rate indicator and a blood pressure monitor, you would be amazed. Your heart is pounding and your blood pressure is soaring. This is one of the reasons why I have such a healthy respect for hitters. Staring down a 90 mile an hour fastball takes guts. Hitting one takes emotional confidence.

Remember this guys: Sound swing fundamentals are just the first step. Obviously a critical first step, but swing mechanics are not what makes contact; your confidence is what allows you to use your great mechanics. If you don't have confidence the best mechanics in the world are worthless.

NOTE: If you're connecting (no pun intended) with the techniques and methods I'm teaching throughout this book, at this point you should be mentally seeing how to handle yourself at the plate. If you're not, don't worry, just go back and read chapters one through five again so you can really burn those concepts into your mind. Your great swing or awesome glove techniques didn't happen overnight and understanding your minds, both of them, and how to manage doubt and fear under pressure is no different. It takes practice and patience.

Each pitch is a new opportunity so look to the future, don't dwell on the past. If you have your little dog under control, and your BIG-Dog is holding the bat, you're going to make contact because you're good and you believe in yourself.

Getting Behind

When you get behind in the count, don't freak out. Just like any other pressure packed situation, control it, don't let it control you. Step out of the batter's box, take

Bloomington, IN: The Indiana Hoosiers in a team huddle before a game against Minnesota. Head Coach Bob Morgan. Photo by Paul Riley, IU Athletics.

control of the rhythm, breathe, and see the pitcher and the field through BIG-Dog Vision. Focus on previous clutch hits, don't hesitate and rip-it.

Finals

If you've made it to finals at state, or any title tournament, you and your teammates are obviously doing a lot of things right. The primary concerns now, more than ever, are avoiding distractions and staying emotionally balanced.

Warning: It's not time to celebrate just because you made it to finals. This is a bad move guys and I've seen it happen too many times. Wait until after finals to release all of that pent-up emotional energy.

Here's the situation: You and your teammates have been committed for months. You're in the finals and it feels great. One more game and the season is over. One more game and it could be the team dog pile in the middle of the field. One more game and you and your teammates could be holding the championship trophy high over your heads. Getting to finals is a tremendous accomplishment and naturally you feel like celebrating.

But wait! Get a grip. Oops. First, I should ask you about your dream. Is your dream to be a state champion or just make it to finals? If it's just to make it to finals, then go celebrate.

The distractions before finals can be the worst. Your emotions are on overload because you actually have a shot at the dream. In a short while you'll be on the field playing high-level ball, maybe in most important game of your competitive life. For many of you, your mind and emotions will be everywhere. Finals are the most important time to keep doing what you've been doing.

The bottom line is, whatever you've been doing the previous couple of days, keep doing it. It's OK to accept congratulations for making it to finals from Grandpa and Grandma, but don't even think for minute you're done. Don't celebrate yet, mentally or otherwise. Don't even look up.

To maintain focus before finals, one of the key problems is dealing with The Stands. They will be packed an hour or so before the game, which means new distractions. Make sure that you keep your Game Mode mindset fully engaged. I'm not suggesting being intensely focused, I'm just saying don't celebrate. Use your Confidence Routines to keep you mind where it needs to be—focused on competing, not socializing and celebrating.

You'll lessen the dramatic swings from confident to doubtful – the composure battle—if you learn how to deal with the transitions and how to keep your mind competitively focused. Once you master these techniques, you'll be able to step-up and compete with confidence. So show some teeth and let your BIG-Dog out!

"When nothing is sure, everything is possible."

— Margaret Drabble

SUMMARY

- Now it's time to play some ball.
- Fight the composure battle in the transitions.
- Stay focused, especially at major tournaments.
- Know when to turn laser beam focus on and off.
- Be aware of dugout dynamics.
- On-deck is when your confidence will get tested.
- Show some teeth and let your BIG-Dog out.

"The battle over composure is fought in the transitions. The transitions are when most of us go nuts, meltdown emotionally, and lose our composure. Stay away from negative what if mental chatter. Master BIG-Dog mental techniques so you can step-up and compete, with confidence." — Steve Knight

Chapter Seven

DREAM • Your Power

There's only one road to a state championship, and it's called d-e-d-i-c-a-t-i-o-n. The road of dedication is driven with discipline, and that is why many players fail—lack of discipline is the giant killer.

So many great athletes – young and old – don't even come close to achieving their potential, because they refuse to discipline themselves.

Over the past few years my house has been full of teenagers and after watching many of them grapple with issues of discipline, I will be the first to acknowledge, it's tough. In our communities today there are all too few living role models for true dedication and discipline. The majority of America's citizens have grown fat, lazy, and unmotivated.

"The future belongs to those who believe in the beauty of their dreams."

— Eleanor Roosevelt

Above: Former Round Rock High School pitcher John Danks steps up to the big league as he tries on his new cap as a Texas Ranger at a press conference at the Ballpark in Arlington, Texas on July 11, 2003.

Left Page: Chagrin Falls, Ohio- Kenston High School player (first) Moone attempts to beat the throw. Photo Kenston High School.

Discipline is almost non-existent in our schools. The "pleasure" options teens have are extensive. The cars, cash, contraband, and girls are constant distractions from real achievement. Everyday athletes are faced with the difficult decision of whether to work or pursue pleasure.

Let me say this: You will progress rapidly in life if you're wise enough to realize that just because something is available, that does not make it a good thing.

Did you get that point? When there is no party to go to, there is no decision to make, that's easy. But when you have options, decisions have to be made. And if you want to distinguish yourself from the average, you have to separate yourself from the pack, because the majority of your peers are totally focused on pleasure.

During your lifetime you won't see or meet very many people who are trying to achieve personal greatness. Why? It's too scary. The majority of people are mentally too weak to make courageous decisions.

As a teenager in America today, separating yourself from your peers to strive and excel, is a courageous decision.

"Wanting to be a state champion is a goal, not a dream. All that you'll get from being a state champion is the dream."

I think at this point it's important that I tell you a little bit about myself, so this chapter doesn't come across too harsh. Or, if it does, you'll understand why.

I would evaluate my athleticism as slightly above average, but am I physically gifted? No. Not in the least.

Physically, I was born a little dog.

My advantages are: 1) I love to practice; I truly enjoy working at getting better at something. When I retired from high-level competitive weight lifting after eleven years I was looking for another sport to challenge myself with, and found golf. I hit two hundred balls every day until I achieved a three handicap. For me that wasn't a grind. That was fun. 2) I've never been highly social. I'm not antisocial, but hanging out and partying was never compelling to me, even as a teenager. So from a training standpoint I've never had to grapple with whether to work or play, train or party. I've always naturally gravitated towards work, not play. But, for many of you that battle is intense and fought with extreme anxiety.

So, someone with my mindset looks at the work or play decision like, "What's your problem? Make the decision. Are you a champion or slacker?"

As my son Nick, who's eighteen, was reading the first draft of this chapter he shook his head and said, "Dad, you still don't get it. You're weird. Most of us don't think like you. For most of us, even if we have a real, tangible dream, forsaking our friends and isolating ourselves to train is like solitary confinement. It's not a simple decision."

I thank my son not only for his perspective, which has helped me better relate to you, but most importantly for his mature delivery.

Many of your coaches, especially those who know how to win, will come across with a similar black or white mindset; you do or you don't. Now, for the first time I realize clearly that for a lot of you, you get stuck in the middle being pulled in both directions.

So, how do I help you find the motivation and discipline to party and socialize less, and work and train more?

Here's the bottom line: as an athlete, especially in high school, you can't have it all. An athlete's commitments are triple that of most non-athletes. Like it or not, if you really want to excel, there isn't enough time to get it all in. The main reason is sleep. For athletes, rest is critical. You train and practice hard, lift weights and condition, and the only way to recover and regenerate is consistent sleep. Partying and "hang-time" cuts into sleep. Why? Because you have to get up at six or seven in the morning to get to school while all of your party buddies are snuggled-in, warm, snoring in their beds. They have nothing to get up for other than the next party. You have a dream.

Pitchers: While this topic relates to all baseball players, this clearly relates to all of you aspiring elite pitchers. Think about it this way, no one is born with the inherent knowledge of how to throw a curve ball, sinker, or slider Those skills are learned. Natural talent and athleticism have little to do with being a successful pitcher. Sure, natural arm strength will help, but how many successful pitchers only throw a fastball? If you want to dominate on the mound, you have to discipline yourself to work hard and develop the physical and mental skills of a competitor. Discipline yourself to put in the repetitions and get the master skills you need to be successful. You'll notice a huge psychological advantage when you're matched up against the staff ace from your archrival, because you know you've put in the time, while he's been partying all winter with his buddies. Not only will you be more capable physically with your pitches and control, your confidence will be much higher because you've figured out how to discipline yourself, which will carry over to your performance on the mound.

So, if you struggle with discipline how do you get some?

First, lets look at the dictionary definition: "dis-ci-pline: activity, exercise, or regimen that develops or improves a skill."

As I'm sure you already know, discipline is not about fun, it's about work.

The only way I know of to possess genuine discipline is to have a real dream. To clearly understand why you're doing what you're doing, why it's important to you, and why nothing is going to get in your way to achieve your dream … absolutely nothing.

When creating your dream it's very important to understand the difference between your dream and your goals. Your dream is not a goal. Where, in visualizing, I've advised not to focus on the rewards, but to focus on the battle, your dream is the opposite; it's all about the rewards. Your dream is what you're going to obtain emotionally from all your dedication, discipline, and hard work.

Too often we only focus on goals, which tend to be bland and tasteless. Your dream is where you find and feel the emotion and all the glory. Goals are short term "markers" on the way forward to accomplishing your dream.

This is where most of you get lost; you don't create a vision for yourself. Think, gentlemen. Picture the future, not just short-term pursuit of pleasure.

Wanting to be a state champion is a goal, not a dream. All that you'll get from being a state champion is the dream.

Example: Most of you want a car. Why? Because you have a variety of mental pictures of what it will be like to have a car: Feeling cool, being free, dating, running around with your buddies. You have all sorts of feelings that go along with having a car. That's a dream.

Working toward a championship has to have the same meanings and feelings, or there's no motivation. Are you seeing it?

Recently I was talking with an old weightlifting buddy, Rick Mooney, in North Carolina. Since we're proud dads, of course we talked mostly about our sons.

His son Will is going to be a senior this year, and is a baseball fanatic. If Will can play year-round he does. He works diligently and consistently at improving his game. He is already getting letters-of-interest from top colleges, and I asked Rick if Will had his sights on the Pros. Rick belly laughed and said, "He lives, eats, and breathes the Pros."

Without even asking Will specifics I know he has a vision of what it will be like to be in the Pros: Catching the big game, throwing a key runner out at second base, maybe even signing the big contract, or blasting a homer to win the series.

It doesn't matter. Whatever Will's specifics are, he has feelings and emotions associated with his dream. They are very real to him and are what drive him forward. Will then sets short-term goals to improve his performance. As he improves, the goals change. But the dream stays the same.

Your Power

Your dream is your power. Ask yourself: Why are you out for baseball? Why put yourself through the practice, training, and hard work? Why do you want to be a champion? What's your dream?

So many of you vacillate between being a stud, and being a contender. Some days you're on, and some days you're off. Some days you have the dream, but most days you don't. OK, yeah, it's fun to party, but what are you really getting out of it other than immediate gratification? Answer: Nothing.

I can only hope that I'm expressing this point with supreme clarity, so you get it. To be able to say "no thanks" to the social opportunities that will present themselves everyday, all day long, and instead go train or prepare requires a dream. The clarity of your dream is what helps you stay dedicated. If you don't have a real dream of why you want to excel, and if those reasons aren't crystal clear, staying committed will be a tremendous challenge, if you can stay committed at all.

Your dream is your power.

Weak no-dream examples: 1. I don't know, it's something to do. 2. Your friends want you on the team. 3. Your dad played baseball. 4. Coach says: "You could be a champion."

Strong BIG-dream examples: 1. Your future is college and you need a scholarship. 2. You want to see how far you can push yourself. 3. You want to prove to yourself and everyone else that you can be great at something. 4. You want to distinguish yourself in our community as an individual who can achieve. 5. Best of all, "you" want to be a champion.

There are many other examples of weak and strong dreams. It is absolutely vital that you have a clear, strong vision of your dream, and yes, everyday it will be a battle—options require making decisions. Again, most Americans have too many pleasure options, and do not make courageous achievement based decisions.

Stanford Cardinals player Brian Hall slides safe into third base. Photo by David Gonzales www.gonzalesphoto.com.

Here's where you might be thinking, "I have my dream, but I still struggle with dedication and discipline." I know that many of you feel that way.

Sacrifice

The conflict lies in that many of you have not embraced, grasped, taken hold of the fact that dedication and discipline mean sacrifice. This is not a lecture; it's reality.

In order to be a champion at anything, you have to do things that elevate yourself above the average, which requires sacrifice. "Sac-ri-fice: the surrender or destruction of something valued for the sake of something having a higher or more pressing claim."

Translation: Less party, more work, equals BIG-Dog status.

Going back to my perspective: I never really had to sacrifice in order to achieve. I didn't really care about partying and socializing, so for me it was hardly a decision. No big sacrifice.

Greensboro,NC:Will Mooney-catcher, R/R, a freshman (2004 season) at Averett University (Danville, VA) shows awesome swing mechanics, and eyes on the ball concentration vs. Greensboro College. Mooney's current batting average is .331, and his high school career (Western Guildford) was .391. The photo bottom right is of Mooney as a Little Leaguer, Age 11. Photos by Terry Storm.

California: Aliso Niquel High School Wolverine hitter Tyler Bowman looks on as team-mate attempts to score. Sommer McCartney Head Coach. Photo by Aliso Niquel Baseball.

For most of you it is a HUGE deal. I have to say, I feel for you. But the reality is, if you're going to excel you have to submit. You have to submit yourself to the reality of striving for excellence. You have to realize that the bottom line is you can't have it all. That's just the way it is. As kids you kick and scream over that reality, not realizing it's the difference between becoming a champion and staying a contender. A champion will submit himself to the sacrifices of training and the pursuit of a higher dream, realizing that in order to acquire the reality of his dream, sacrifices have to be made.

Personal story: Recently I was involved with a high school senior who is a gifted athlete, physically. He played a variety of sports since the time he was a puppy. Football and basketball ended up being his two primary interests.

When he got to high school he was heading down the party road, and by his sophomore year he was pretty much self-destructing. His junior year was a disaster; academically he was a no-show, and, of course, he was ineligible.

He had been a friend of my youngest son for years. The summer before his senior year we ran into him. After sharing his personal story we offered to take him in, hoping that a fresh start and new environment would help him get back on track to finish high school, and ultimately go to college.

At first, he was negative and reluctant. He thought he was too far behind, besides, there was no guarantee he would be eligible. I told him that assuming things in life was … well … ignorant, and suggested that with a couple of investigative phone calls he would know exactly what his options were. He agreed, and within a couple of calls we found out that he could enroll and he was eligible. He moved in with us, agreeing to my one condition; that he had to go to school, no excuses. If he didn't, he'd have to move out.

He was pumped, back in school and on the football field again. Practice went great, and he quickly earned a starting position as a corner. He contributed in the first couple of games and was looking forward to a great season. Then the phone call came.

I had kept in what I thought was pretty close contact with him regarding his school attendance and what I heard was, "Are you kidding, I'm going to every class. Why would I blow this?"

He lied. The Athletic Director told me he had been skipping class since the first day of school. His attendance record was barely 50%.

It was a sad day for me; unfortunately I had to ask him to move out. I genuinely cared about this kid, and wanted to do all that I could for him. To keep up his end of the deal all that he had to do was go to class. There were no grade requirements … just go to class.

As I was discussing with him why he chose to skip school and blow this opportunity he looked at me like I was some sort of idiot and said, "Because I want to have fun."

I'll never forget that. Fun, at the expense of everything.

For whatever reason, it was more important for this young man to identify, connect with, and relate to kids who wanted to party vs. the kids who wanted to excel. He made a decision, and now he has to live with it.

Trust me gentlemen, like it or not, dedication, discipline, and sacrifice will have to be your best friend if you want to excel.

Inspiration: Turn to page 130. and read John Dank's interview. John was drafted in the first round (2003) by the Texas Rangers, and encourages all of you to "believe in yourself before anyone else does," and "work hard and don't give up."

The Schedule

Once you decide, with conviction, that you can sacrifice certain social pleasures for a higher dream, and that you can separate yourself from the "pleasure" pack, I strongly recommend putting together a daily/weekly schedule to give yourself a framework to operate within. It can be as detailed as you like, which depends on your personality type. But, give yourself a daily/weekly look at what you need to do, along with what you want to do.

If you just take a little time to plan, you'll still be able to get some "hang-time" in, just not as much as your party friends. That's why you'll become a champion, and they won't. It truly is your decision.

G-Man Baseball Little Leaguer sets-up for the throw. Photo source www.community-webshots.com.

Training

This can be a short section. You know what your daily training chores are, so like Nike says, "Just Do It."

The Test

Over the course of the season many times you'll be confronted with "do you" or "don't you" decisions. Do you get up and go to school, or sleep-in? Do you blow off scheduled preparation, or go hangout? Do you stay out late and party, or go home and rest up for tomorrow's training? Each one of those decisions is a test.

Your party "friends" will provide added pressure; "Come on man, just hangout." And of course, you'll want to, which isn't a bad thing; you're human. But each time you let partying cut into your training and preparation you're jeopardizing the potential of becoming a unique member of "our" championship community—those who can submit themselves to the sacrifices for higher achievements.

No doubt your decision record won't be perfect when the season is over. That's OK. I encourage you to make more positive decisions than negative. Make more decisions that will propel you towards your dream, rather than trap you among the average.

Your dream is your power. Your conviction to do what is necessary to achieve your dream, day in and day out, is what will make you a champion. Remember: The road to being a champion is the road of dedication, discipline, and sacrifice—you can do it—dream and commit!

110% Effort

Notice that I haven't even mentioned, "give it your all." Give everything you do 110% percent. Go, go, go, and go some more.

Intensity of effort is another deal. That comes from your personal drive, your BIG-Dog factor.

Personally, I would rather see young athletes give 90% effort 100% of the time, as opposed to 110% effort 80% of the time. The great champions of course give 200% effort every single waking, breathing moment.

Dream BIG

Without a vivid picture of a real dream, it doesn't matter who tries to push you, you won't have consistent motivation to make difficult social decisions, which will jeopardize your chances of achieve success. Give yourself the opportunity to better yourself by creating a dream, and committing to the dedication, discipline, and sacrifice required.

Dream BIG, it's your power.

SUMMARY

- ◆ Dedication leads to accomplishment.
- ◆ Separate yourself from the pleasure pack; make courageous decisions.
- ◆ Submit to the sacrifices of achievement.
- ◆ Everyday it's a battle; options demand decisions.
- ◆ Improve your discipline; stay on task.
- ◆ Dream your future. Define your goals.
- ◆ Dream BIG. Create your power.

"I don't know of many instances when someone accomplished something of significance without first dreaming about it, and then committing to what was required to accomplish the task. I encourage all of you to dream, and commit." — Steve Knight

Championship
Interviews

**12 nationally ranked teams and players
share great advice, inspiring stories, and
personal photos.**

**Special thanks to the coaches and players for their advice,
stories, and photos; and to Anthony Maggio for doing an
outstanding job producing, assembling, and writing the
interview section.**

SETON HALL

New Jersey

Parochial "A" state champs 23 times, including three of last four

Seton Hall Pirates
West Orange, New Jersey

Head Coach: Mike Sheppard Jr.

Assistants: Frank Gately, Paul Gizzo, Kurt Buehlmaier, John McIntee, Dave Kahney, Fr. Stephen Kilcarr

Advice to coaches

"As far as advice for coaches/teams trying to build a winning program, it must all begin with a coach's philosophy for his program. The coach must establish a philosophy and get his players to believe in it. Our philosophy is divided into for areas of importance in order to achieve success.

They are:

1. Demonstrate sportsmanship
Act like a gentleman before, during and after the ball game. Be humble in victory, gracious in defeat. Treat opponents with respect. Abide by the rules of the game. Respect the decisions and judgments of umpires without argument. Refrain from using obscenities or profanities. Exercise self-control at all times. The greatest opportunities for sportsmanlike conduct arise where there are the greatest opportunities for unsportsmanlike conduct.

2. Striving to win/striving for excellence
Although winning is important, it is not the sole purpose for your involvement in our program. Playing to win, within the rules and the spirit of the game is what we expect. The will to win is not nearly as important as the will to prepare to win (work ethic). You are not a "loser" as long as you have given your all (mentally/physically/emotionally) and have preformed to the best of your ability. Winning must be kept in perspective. It should never be encouraged at the cost of sportsmanship, discipline, integrity and respect for the game, opponents and umpires.

3. Striving for consistency.

Roster 2003

2B - Ryan Clark, DH - Rich Goulian, 3B - Eric Duncan, SS - Rob Clark, LF - Joe Russo, 1B Chris Cancro, RF - Steve Fordyce, C - Matt Halligan, CF Nick Christiani, P - Javier Martinez, Steve Brennan, Nick Christiani, Dan Merklinger, Rich Goulian

Consistency is the most accurate gauge for personal and team performance. It is the ability to perform to the best of your ability day after day throughout the season. A team that performs consistently will come out victorious most of the time.

4. Commit yourself
Commitment is a willingness to work hard due to your devotion to your teammates, team goals, and self-improvement. Teamwork is nothing more than everybody being committed to each other's success."

School history

- Eight Greater Newark Tournament titles, including five of last seven.
- 10 Iron Division titles, including five of last six.
- 23 Parochial "A" state championships, including three of last four.

2003 accomplishments

- Greater Newark Tournament Champions
- Iron Division Champions
- Parochial "A" North and Overall State Champions
- Ranked No. 1 in New Jersey, No. 9 in United States by Baseball Coaches of America

2003 stats

- 30-1 overall record
- .387 team batting average
- 300 runs scored to opponents' 60
- .498 team on base percentage
- 1.46 team ERA
- 223 strikeouts as a pitching staff

Above/Top: The Pirates play a game of pepper during pre-game. Middle: The Pirates pose with the 2003 state championship trophy. Bottom: Second baseman Ryan Clark waits for a throw to tag out the runner.
Left Page/Left: Coach Sheppard hugs a Pirates' player while the team celebrates the state championship. Right: Javier Martinez (9-0 record) makes a pitch.

CHAPARRAL

Arizona

Four-time state champs, regional champs 18 times since 1975

Chaparral Firebirds
Scottsdale, Arizona

**Head Coach:
Jerry Dawson**

assistants: Mike Miller, Tim Rondina, Chuck McAdoo

Q: What was your best high school baseball moment?

"I coached for 20 years before we won our first state championship and 25 years before we got our first player into the major leagues of baseball. Both those things stand out as special in my memory. In 1994 our club had 30 wins and 4 losses and were state champs with a 9 - 0 win over Tucson Sunnyside in the championship game. That club featured current Chicago White Sox first baseman Paul Konerko. While he was the centerpiece of an outstanding club, there were many quality players that surrounded him. Shaking the hand of my long time assistant coach, Mark Miller - 19 years, and knowing that we had finally reached a goal that we had sought after for so long - was a very

special moment. Mark is a special man who is still coaching with me. He will return for his 30th year as an assistant this year. The bond we have is strong and he is a great teacher of the game with a love of the game that is unsurpassed. Obviously, that was a special group of young men and the memory of each I will always treasure, but the bond developed with another adult who shares the same goals as yourself, the same passion for the game and works with you to attain those goals is very special.

A second very special memory for me is the night of August 31, 1997. At about 11:30 pm the phone at my home rang. As I staggered thru the darkness I was wondering who would be calling at that late hour and how such calls are never good news. The first words out of the

Roster 2003

OF - Ryan Weimar, SS - Austin Yount, OF - Ryan Davis, P - Greg Abram, OF - Curt Miaso, C - Andrew Gulla, OF/3B - Ben Robinson, P - David Cross, 3B - Michael Levi, 2B - Michael Lio, P - Jason Corley, P/1B - Ike Davis, 1B - Tim Sherlock, P/DH - Chris Cox

person on the other end were, "Coach, I got the call." Half asleep I failed to recognize the voice of the caller and certainly the sentence made no sense. After mumbling some incoherent reply, the caller was nice enough to expand by saying, "Coach its Paul, I got the call to meet the big club in Arlington (Tex.) tomorrow night." I remember the goose bumps on my arms at that moment very vividly. I also remember the same goose bumps as I sat in the stands at Arlington stadium in Texas and watched him enter the field with the Los Angeles Dodgers for batting practice the next night. I had decided to try to attend that game at the last moment and had been lucky enough to find flight connections. Because of the lateness of the planning and execution of the trip, I was unable to notify Paul that I was coming. He was traveling also and communication was impossible. I remember vividly the look on his face when i was first able to make eye contact with him as he was running during pregame in the outfield. It was a special moment in time for me – one I am sure he has long forgotten but I will never forget. We had so many players get as high as Triple-A baseball but none had ever gotten to make the final step to the big leagues. I was so very happy for him."

Above: Jerry Dawson holds a pregame meeting prior to taking the field for the championship game.
Left Page: Firebirds celebrate after winning a 12 inning, 4.5 hour marathon game.

2003 accomplishments

- State champs
- Ranked 13th in BCA poll

Team history

- Four state championships
- 18 East Sky region championships since 1975
- 100 players have gone on to play collegiate or professional baseball, including six players selected by USA Baseball to play in the international World Championships
- Four-time state runner-up

Advice to coaches

"There are four areas where I would offer advice to young people wanting to enter coaching as a profession. Developing a plan for your coaching is a must. That sounds so simple but when you break down a sport like baseball it becomes much more complicated. One needs to take each skill area and devise a comprehensive plan for teaching and refining each of the skills involved. Not only must you teach skills, but you must also develop and teach a system of play. Being able to put nine players on the field that can work within a defined system and trust each other and that system is a must. Organization is also big. Time management becomes a huge problem because of the number of skills and team concepts to be taught and then refined. You need to prioritize the teaching areas relating to your philosophy as it relates to their importance to you. Too many young people are coming into coaching today for the fun of winning. Every game that has a winner also must have a loser, so a willingness to work hard is a must. The hours are long, the work can be physically demanding, and the pay in terms of dollars is small. If coaches don't possess a passion for teaching the game their careers are short lived. Lastly, never stop trying to improve as a coach. You can never know it all and the moment you feel you do it is time to find another profession. Clinics, conferences and talking the sport and the teaching of that sport are a must if you are to continue to evolve as a professional. One must continually strive to improve their presentation, organizational skills and knowledge of the sport in question."

Above/Top: Austin Yount, nephew of Hall of Famer Robin Yount. Middle: Curt Miaso lines a single to right-center field in the championship game. Bottom: Firebirds lined up during pregame ceremonies at the championship game.
Left Page/Top: Championship game winning pitcher Greg Abram. Middle: The 2003 seniors. Bottom: Catcher Andrew Gulla waits on deck.

ELKINS

Texas

Back-to-back state champions, four straight region titles - six overall

Elkins Knights
Sugar Land, Texas

Head Coach:
Rick Carpenter (center)

Assistants: Richard Thistlethwaite, Tony Mardirosian, Jody Albright, Ron Beard

Q: What was your best high school baseball moment?

"It's hard to narrow it down, but the first state championship we won when that final out was recorded, that was a huge thrill. To get to the pinnacle of your career in what you're trying to accomplish. That was in 1995. We've had the opportunity to win three overall. They've all had different meanings. The second one we won was in 2002 and that made us national champs in USA Today and Baseball America. That was a big event too. Not only was it a state championship but a national crown is hard to put into words because it is such a high.

Last year when we won it, the fact it was back-to-back was special and we also really overachieved. All three of those moments are my favorites. They all had different meanings and were big deals."

Roster 2003

C - Grant Taylor, 1B - Kelly Shearer or Michael Susaneck, 2B - Chad Huffman, SS - Will Carpenter, 3B - Matt Carpenter, LF - Adam Perry, CF - Spencer Jackson, RF - Chris Fewell, DH - Chris Morris, P - Shearer, Susaneck, Stephen Porlier

Advice to coaches

"Well, obviously you have to have a few factors that you have no control over. You have to be in an area with decent kids. But it doesn't matter where you are, I certainly once had a job at a place that was not known for baseball and was a slow economical place not conducive to baseball. Basically, if you want to develop an outstanding program you have to eat, sleep and drink it. The philosophy I go by in my own mind is that I'm always trying to outwork my biggest competitor. I preach that to the kids too. I try to live by the fact that you're not doing anything today if you're thinking about what you did yesterday. You have to try to improve every day. It takes a major commitment. Its just not for works hours only, you have to take work home with you. I don't think you'll find a program in America that wins where that is not the case."

School history

- 10 seasons of varsity competition
- Three state championships
- Four straight region titles, six overall
- Seven district championships
- 10 playoff appearances
- 10 players drafted by MLB
- 2002 national champions

2003 accomplishments

- Ranked 14th in nation by BCA
- district, region and state champions

2003 stats

- 31-8 overall record
- .326 team batting average
- 38 home runs
- 289 runs in 39 games
- 54 errors all season
- 1.69 team ERA
- 321 strikeouts in 248 innings pitched
- 60 earned runs allowed

Above/Top: Knights going through their pre-game ritual. Bottom: Chad Huffman being greeted at home in the state championship game.

Left Page/Middle: Jody Albright, Kelly Shearer and Tony Mardirosian chatting on their way to the dugout. Bottom: The Knights celebrating after the final out of the state championship game at Minute Maid Park.

LA COSTA CANYON

California

Set CIF record with 32 wins in one season en route to state title

Q: What was your best high school baseball moment?

"The most memorable high school baseball experience was winning the California Interscholastic Federation Division I title in San Diego, Calif. A lot of different records were on the line. If we were to win we (La Costa Canyon Mavericks) would become the winningest high school baseball team in the history of San Diego (32-1). We would also break the record for most consecutive wins at 27, a streak that is still going. We would become the California State Team of the Year, as well as the National Champions in one poll. To achieve all this we had to beat the most dominant team in San Diego over the past ten years - Rancho Bernardo - that was making its fifth straight appearance in the championship. It was a rainy night in San Diego and the lead had changed hands a few times. Both teams came out firing and were not going to let up no matter what Mother Nature threw at them. At the end of seven the score was tied at 4-4. We took the field in the eighth inning and Rancho Bernardo began to rally. With two outs

La Costa Canyon Mavericks
Carlsbad, California

Head Coach:
Justin Machado

assistant coaches: Rudy Rodriguez, Tim Kechter, Mark Miller

and men on second and third they hit a shot into deep left field only to be caught. The Mavericks came out in the bottom half and started a rally of their own. With one out and men on first and second, Michael Scharbarth hit a slow roller to the third baseman. The third baseman fielded the ball and threw it wildly up the line eventually ending up in left field. The runner on second rounded third and scored on the errant throw. Once that run scored and the game had ended a wild celebration occurred at home plate. It was like a

Roster 2003

CF - Andrew Nacario, SS - Joey Burke, 2B - Chris Fuller, LF - Michael Scharbarth, 1B - Johnny Zepeda, C - Scott Clement, 3B - Nick Diehl, DH - Peter Betea, RF - Nick Burke, P - Doug Konoske, Michael Kenney, Drew Logan, Travis Goldbach, Brian Brehm

huge weight had been lifted off our shoulders. So many records and rankings were at stake that it was nice to see such a great group of individuals achieve the ultimate goal."

Advice to coaches

"If I were to give advice to other coaches it would be to not worry about wins and losses. Create a program that builds responsibility and accountability in student-athletes. The greatest thing we as coaches can do for our players is to stress education and its importance. In the long run most people will never remember what your record was in any given year but they will be able to relate your program to producing strong citizens in the community. Wins and losses will come with talent that you are given in any given year. As a coach, if you have created an atmosphere that demands success through responsibility and accountability, your players will rise to the occasion."

School history

- Seven seasons of varsity competition
- Five Avocado League Championships
- Five Pirate/Falcon Tournament championships
- Two North County Tournament championships
- One San Diego Lions Tournament Classic Division championship

2003 accomplishments

- CIF Division I champions
- CIF record with 32 wins in one season
- Ranked fifth in nation by BCA

2003 stats

- 32-1 overall record
- .371 team batting average
- .482 team on-base percentage
- 274 runs scored
- 2.01 team ERA
- Struck out 181 batters

Above/Left: The Mavericks watch in anticipation during the state championship game. Right: Mavericks stand at attention during the national anthem.

Left Page/Left: Nick Burke makes a diving catch in right field to save the victory in the CIF semi-finals. Right: The Mavericks celebrate at home plate after their victory against Rancho Bernardo at Tony Gywnn Stadium to win the CIF Division I title.

LA CUEVA

New Mexico

Went 29-0 to give La Cueva its first state championship

La Cueva Bears
Albuquerque, New Mexico

Head Coach: Stan McCeever

assistants (left to right): Rob Hicks, Rick Ingle, Curt Johnson

Q: What was your best high school baseball moment?

"My best high school baseball moment happened in May of 1998. I was the head coach at Del Norte High School in Albuquerque. When I arrived at Del Norte in 1993, my first high school head baseball coaching job, it was easily the most down and out high school program in the city.

Over the course of the next six years we steadily built up the program into a contender and a consistent state tournament qualifier. In May of 1998 I took a group of kids to the state tournament that had totally bought into our program and the team concept. This group of kids allowed me to be their coach, no outside influences. We played together as a team, spring and summer, for years. Del Norte High School was the smallest AAAA school in the state and a berth in a state championship game in any sport was pretty much unheard of and hasn't occurred again since.

Our team won in the round of sixteen in our last at bat and again in the quarterfinals in our last at bat. In the semifinals, we trailed 2-1 going into the bottom of the seventh. With one out we proceeded to get three straight singles and tie the game. Up came Paul Garcia, nicknamed "little oso" (little bear in Spanish), our first baseman. On a 1-0 count, Paul hit a homerun over the right center-field fence of the Albuquerque Dukes Stadium to win it and put us into the state championship game. I will never forget how excited the boys and our fans were and how much that accomplishment meant to them. I have never felt more satisfaction as a coach, more proud of a team, and have never enjoyed a bus ride back to school as much as I did that day. Although we lost the next day, I will never feel more close to a group of kids as I did the Knights in 1998.

My dream of winning a state championship finally came true in 2003. My Bears team finished the season 29-0 and ranked as high as sixth in the nation in one poll. This was a big moment in my coaching career as well. One might think that winning the state championship would have to be the biggest moment in my career, but the underdog Knights of 1998 and their total dedication to me, to each other and to our program is the most special thing that I have experienced in coaching."

Roster 2003

DH - Matt Quillen, 2B - Jordan Pacheco, C - Zach Arnett, OF - Cameron House, OF - Seth Johnson, Utl Inf. - James Parr, OF - Ramon Romero, SS - Tavo Hall, 1B - Billy Hogan, 3B - Andrew Salas, P - Kevin Biringer, Brad Copass, Pacheco, House, Parr

Advice to coaches

"1. Be an educated coach (i.e. learn from others, clinics, etc.) and teach what you believe in.
2. As hard as it may be, be positive and be patient.
3. You don't have to yell and curse to be a good coach.
4. Be totally honest with pro scouts, college coaches, assistant coaches, the administration, players, and parents.
5. Maintain a top-notch facility. Your efforts will be appreciated.
6. Hire "good people" as your assistant coaches. The integrity and morals of you and your staff are important.
7. Work hard as a coach. Be organized and make good use of your time. You can't expect your kids to hustle if you won't.
8. Stress the importance of the process of becoming a champion and the championships will take care of themselves."

2003 accomplishments

- Class AAAAA state champs
- Set single season records in wins, runs, and home runs
- Seven players named first team All-State
- Ranked eighth in nation by BCA

2003 stats

- 29-0 record
- scored 374 runs
- hit 79 home runs

Above: The 2003 New Mexico Class AAAAA champion La Cueva Bears.

RIVERSIDE

South Carolina

Four-time state champs, have won nine straight conference titles

Q: What was your best high school baseball moment?

"After going 20-0 to start the season, we lost the championship game of the Southeastern Baseball Classic in one of the best-played games I have ever seen. The teams shook hands and we went to the outfield to discuss the game as always. When I addressed the team there was a sense of shock and disappointment, but more than ever there was a sense of relief. The streak was over - we could now relax and refocus. A loss is never good, but we took the loss and redirected it to a positive and were determined it would not happen again. At that point, I felt certain that we would rebound and play better than we had the previous week.
We made it to the state championship best of three series, and after winning the first game 7-3, we won the second game 11-1 in six innings to win the AAA state championship.
So, with all that said the best moment of the year was the last pitch of that game.

Riverside Warriors
Greer, South Carolina

Head Coach: Chris Bates

assistants: Mark Kish, Tom Myers

All year the players were very focused and businesslike in each victory. These players had all been in big games, but had never won a championship of this magnitude. I told them that it would be a feeling that they would never forget and they sort of played it off like it would just be another game. As the game began to get lopsided, I too was wondering if it would be as meaningful or as exciting. With two outs and two strikes on the batter in the bottom of the sixth, the players began to stand at the edge of the dugout-they were getting that feeling. The pitch was thrown, the batter swung and missed and those businesslike/focused players turned in to the happiest young men on top of each in the middle of the field-a dogpile. All the pressures of winning it all that we had heard all year had been relieved and the marathon was com-

Roster 2003

C - Kyle Enders, CF - Brad Chalk, RF - Brad Hocking, SS - Andrew Crisp, LF - Adam Crisp, 1B - Adam Wood, 3B - Will Kish, 2B - Jordan Mitchell, P - Marc Young, Andrew Farotto, Chalk, Hocking,

plete.
This was all possible through hard work and determination to be the best. These guys would not be denied because they believed in one another and the system. I have never been prouder of a group of young men. They carried themselves as champions on and off the field."

2003 accomplishments

- AAA state champions
- Ranked fourth in BCA poll
- Conference champions

2003 stats

- 29-1 record
- Outscored opponents 283-44.
- Maintained 30-game conference win streak
- .375 team batting average
- .482 team on-base percentage
- .956 team fielding percentage
- 1.217 team ERA
- Struck out 264 batters

Advice to coaches

"The best advice that I have on building a winning program is to develop a philosophy and stick with it. The players must believe in the system that is in place. Practice all situations and explain to them why they are doing this drill or that situation-not just because you said to."

School history

- Four-time state champions
- Nine straight conference championships
- Five-time upper state champions

Above/Top: Fans fill the bleachers behind home plate at a Riverside game. Bottom: The Warriors pose with the state championship trophy.

Left Page/The Warriors celebrate on the field after winning the state championship.

Signed letter of intent to pitch for the University of South Carolina

Brad Hocking

Riverside High School
Greer, South Carolina

Date of Birth: February 21, 1986
Height: 6'2"
Weight: 210 lbs.
Bats: right
Throws: right

Pitcher

Q: What was your best high school baseball moment?

"The most satisfying moment in my many years of baseball was winning the South Carolina State Championship last season. The Championship was a culmination of countless hours of conditioning, weightlifting, and practicing. My love for baseball is greatly based on the team aspect of the game, so winning that trophy overshadows all of my personal accomplishments.

Having pitched in our victorious series opener, I played right field in the second game of the State Championship. It seemed like an ordinary game until the last inning, when the whole experience finally struck me. I often wondered as a

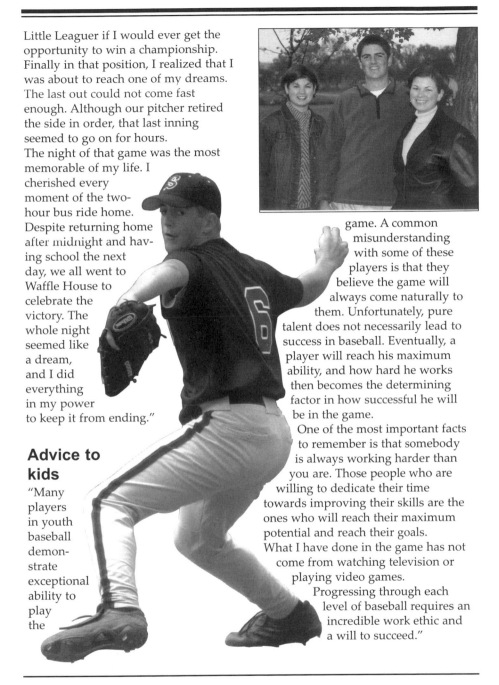

Little Leaguer if I would ever get the opportunity to win a championship. Finally in that position, I realized that I was about to reach one of my dreams. The last out could not come fast enough. Although our pitcher retired the side in order, that last inning seemed to go on for hours.

The night of that game was the most memorable of my life. I cherished every moment of the two-hour bus ride home. Despite returning home after midnight and having school the next day, we all went to Waffle House to celebrate the victory. The whole night seemed like a dream, and I did everything in my power to keep it from ending."

Advice to kids

"Many players in youth baseball demonstrate exceptional ability to play the game. A common misunderstanding with some of these players is that they believe the game will always come naturally to them. Unfortunately, pure talent does not necessarily lead to success in baseball. Eventually, a player will reach his maximum ability, and how hard he works then becomes the determining factor in how successful he will be in the game.

One of the most important facts to remember is that somebody is always working harder than you are. Those people who are willing to dedicate their time towards improving their skills are the ones who will reach their maximum potential and reach their goals.

What I have done in the game has not come from watching television or playing video games. Progressing through each level of baseball requires an incredible work ethic and a will to succeed."

Above/Top: Brad with his sisters Marcie (left) and Erin. Middle: Brad pitching in AAU National Championships in Knoxville, Tennessee.

Left Page: Brad, Asher Hoffman, Will Fitzgerald, Blaine Hart, Taylor Harbin, and Ben Hines taking batting practice on the beach at the World Wood Bat Underclassman Tournament in Jupiter, Florida.

Junior year statistics

- 10-0 record
- .966 ERA
- 83 strikeouts to 12 walks in 58 innings
- .139 batting average against
- .381 batting average
- .480 on base percentage
- 24 RBIs
- Nine doubles

Awards

- Greer Citizen Spring Athlete of the Year
- All-Conference
- High School Sports Report All-State
- AAA State Player of the Year
- SC Baseball Coaches Association All-State
- AAA All-State

Academics

- 1450 SAT score
- 5.1 GPA on four point scale
- Class rank 1 of 281

Q. What was your most clutch performance and how did you handle the situation.

"My most clutch moment in baseball came in the first game of the 2003 South Carolina state championship series. For over a month I had experienced pain in my throwing shoulder. I went to see an orthopedist and the x-rays were negative. The doctor told me that I could do no further damage to my arm by pitching one more game. While warming up before the game, the extreme pain had me doubting that I would be able to play at all, but I told myself that I couldn't let my teammates down in the biggest game of the season. Remembering that the doctor said I would likely cause no further harm to my shoulder, I pitched through the pain. Every pitch was a struggle, but I kept my focus and did everything in my power to give us a chance to win. The pressure of the situation was immense. The overflowing home crowd made the most important game of my life even more intense. The biggest key was treating it like any other game. I went through the same routine, and I didn't try to do anything outside of my ability. I managed to last six innings, and we pulled out the victory, 7-2.

After the season was complete, an MRI showed that I needed surgery for a torn labrum. Although I was upset about the injury, I had the satisfaction of knowing that I contributed to the team's goal of winning the state championship. I would never recommend that anyone pitch through an injury, but I learned the lesson that nothing comes easy in baseball. When faced with obstacles, it takes hard work and dedication to overcome these challenges."

Above/Top: Brad at an Atlanta Thrashers game with friends Andy Mayo, Chris Johnson and Matt Mayo. Bottom: Brad with his dad, Scott, after a Riverside game.

Left Page/Top: Brad at bat for his summer league team, the South Carolina Spirit. Bottom: Brad pitching for the South Carolina Spirit.

FULTON

Virginia

Third-round pick of 2003 Major League Baseball Draft by Florida

Q: What was your best high school baseball moment?

"Through my little league and high school years, I've had a lot of memorable moments. Homeruns, game winning hits, and great plays, but the thing that stands out most in my mind about my high school baseball career was a game I had during the summer of my 11th grade year. I was starting to get a little exposure and the report on me was that I had a good body but I was too big to play shortstop and I was only a good pull hitter. After my junior high school season, I worked extremely hard to prove that I could play short and hit to all parts of the field. I lost 10 pounds of fat in two months, took 250 ground balls a day, went from running a 6.8 in the 60 yard dash to a 6.6, and I worked hours on hitting to the opposite field. In August, I had a showcase game in front of 500 pro scouts and college coaches. My first at bat I hit a triple off the right center field wall followed up with two singles to right field. I also made 6 plays in the field; only one of those balls was routine! After that game and that weekend of competition, I was ranked the number one shortstop in the nation for the class of 2003 according to Baseball America and USA today. It was at that moment I realized that, with persistence, I could overcome negative opinions and criticisms that athletes sometimes feel and hear. That was a very important discovery for me."

Jonathan Fulton

George Washington High School
Danville, Virginia

Date of Birth: December 1, 1983
Height: 6'4"
Weight: 200 lbs.
Bats: right
Throws: right

Shortstop

Junior year statistics
- .433 batting average
- 6 home runs
- 37 RBIs

Senior year
- named USA Today All-American

Advice to kids

"I decided long ago that if I wanted something bad enough all I had to do was work a little harder and I could achieve my goals. When I was in the ninth grade, I was told I could not make the varsity basketball team and I did it. In the 10th grade, I was told I was not strong enough to play football and I became an all-state quarterback with scholarship offers from numerous Division I schools and, finally, when I was 10 years old, I was told I would not ever play professional baseball. I am currently employed by the Florida Marlins. So my advice to all future stars is to work hard, play hard, and REFUSE to give up on your dreams."

Above/Top: Jon with his siblings Peyton, Ben, Joshua, Morgan and Victoria. Middle: Jon with his girlfriend Meredith. Bottom: Jon with friends on draft day.

Left Page: Jon flips the ball to second in a game senior year (photo by Bill Setliff).

STEWART

California

First-round pick of 2003 Major League Baseball Draft by Colorado

Ian Stewart

La Quinta High School
Westminster, California

Date of Birth: April 5, 1985
Height: 6'3"
Weight: 210 lbs.
Bats: left
Throws: right

Q: What was your best high school baseball moment?

"I would have to say that with out a doubt, winning the California Interscholastic Federation Southern Section Division 4 Title was my All-Time favorite moment. I will never forget that day - walking out onto the Anaheim Stadium infield knowing that this would be my last high school game ever. Everything we had worked for during the year, for all the times we hustled down the line to beat out a throw, it was all going to come down to this last game. To make the game even more exciting we were facing our arch rival team from within our league - the Pacifica Mariners. I grew up playing with about 90 percent of their players, which made it a very emotional game. We scored the first, making the score 2-0. Pacifica rallied and came within one run in the top half of the sixth. They held us scoreless in our half of the sixth making for what would be an incredible finish. Their lead off man singled in the top of the seventh and the eighth hitter attempted a sacrifice bunt.

The ninth hitter then struck out on three pitches. That brought up Pacifica's most dangerous hitter - Travis Bernard. He already had a single and a triple. Our pitcher really came after him and got him into a 1-2 count. On the very next pitch, the runner took off. I immediately knew that this guy was going to be hosed with the gun that our catcher, Aaron Randall, had. BAM! Our shortstop Blake Crosby slapped the tag on the runner and the game was over! I immediately sprinted over to my best friend Blake and we jumped into each other's arms and went crazy. All our hard work had paid off and we finally got our well-deserved 'RING.'"

Advice to kids

"I can honestly say that succeeding in baseball starts in the classroom and is carried over onto the baseball field. By doing your homework, going to class, and listening to your teachers you develop incredible habits that are carried over into practice or maybe a game if you have one that day. School and baseball are very similar. To succeed in school you need to listen to your teachers and take their advice when you are learning. When they tell you to go home and practice your math problems or whatever it may be, you need to do that! They know best. I am faithful in my opinion that success starts in the classroom and here's why: Like in the classroom, you need to do your homework and practice it. On the baseball field your homework is to continue to take ground balls everyday. Hit whenever you can and run to stay in shape. You can't improve yourself unless you are dedicated to improving your weaknesses and maintaining your strengths. When your coach/teacher makes suggestions to you, practice hitting the other way, fielding backhands, running the bases, etc., you need to take

that advice and listen to him just as you would in the classroom. Have RESPECT for your teachers/coaches so that you may in return receive their respect."

Above/Top: Ian rounds third in a game for the USA Junior National Team in 2002. Middle: Ian on graduation day with his mother Cindy and father Steve.

Bottom-Left: Ian with his friends Nick DuRee (middle) and Scott Bowling (right). Bottom-Right: Ian leads off first against Mater Dei HIGH ScHOOL at Cal State-Fullerton his senior year.

Senior year statistics

- .487 batting average
- 16 homeruns
- 65 RBIs
- 13 doubles
- 10 stolen bases
- 30 walks

High school awards

- Garden Grove All-League First Team
- Garden Grove League MVP
- Orange County HS Player of the Year
- LA Times HS Player of the Year
- CIF Division 4 Player of the Year
- California State Player of the Year
- All District 8 Player of the Year
- Baseball Coaches Association Player of the Year
- 2003 Louisville Slugger All-American and Player of the Year
- Baseball America All American First Team
- USA Today All-American
- Hammer Strength Player of the Year...
- Cal Hi Sports "Mr. Baseball" 2003
- 16HR and 65RBI set single season record in a season for Orange County
- No. 6 retired by La Quinta High School

Q. What was your most clutch performance and how did you handle the situation.

"My most clutch moment was undoubtedly my game winning homerun in the state playoffs two years ago. We were playing Lompoc High School at our field in the semi-finals of the State Championships. The game was definitely on the line and all I was thinking about was putting the ball in play somewhere. You can't think about trying to hit that game-winning home run because it just won't happen. Before

every at bat I say the same bible verse, which keeps me very calm, yet confident. "I can do all things through Christ who strengthens me." It is Philippians 4:13. When I got into the batters box, I remember taking big, deep breaths to keep me calm as well. I came up in the bottom of the sixth with one out, men on first and second base and we were down by two. I remember the pitcher getting ahead of me early in the count at 0-2. When I fell behind I just kept telling myself, "Stay within your abilities, keep doing what you have been doing all year." You have to think confident in tight situations or you'll just find yourself scared or nervous and won't be able to concentrate on the task at hand. On the 0-2 pitch, he hung a curveball that I blasted over the left-center field fence for what ended up being the

game-winning home run. Our pitcher came shut the team down in the top of the seventh and gave us the win. My home run helped send our team to the State Championships."

Above/Top: is Ian's brother-in-law Jeff, his sister Katie and their son Josh and daughter Emily. Bottom: Ian with high school teammates Aaron Randall (left), Blake Crosby (middle-right), and Ryan Johnson (right).

Left Page/Top: Ian with rookie league teammate Casey Fuller. Bottom: Ian with rookie league teammates Darric Merrel (left), Scott Beerer (middle-right), and John Restrepo (right).

DUCCAN

New Jersey

First-round pick of 2003 Major League Baseball Draft by New York Yankees

Q: What was your best high school baseball moment?

"Choosing the "best" moment in a season filled with great moments is nearly impossible. But the day that really stands out is June 3rd. That was the day of the 2003 Amateur Baseball Draft and the day we played St. Joseph for the North Parochial "A" championship. The pitcher for St. Joseph was the returning pitcher of the year for New Jersey and was again having a great season. He also said in the media that he wanted to face me. The draft began at about noon and I remember huddling around a computer with my family and some of my teammates. The Yankees selected me with the 27th pick overall and I was overjoyed, but realized we had to leave to go play the biggest game of our season against St. Joseph. When we got to the field it was raining -- wonderful. In my first at bat I lined out to the second baseman. I struck out my second at bat and came up again in the fifth inning with my team up 4-3 and two

Eric Duncan

Seton Hall Preparatory School
West Orange, New Jersey

Date of Birth: December 7, 1984
Height: 6'2"
Weight: 195 pounds
Bats: left
Throws: right

Third Baseman

men on base. With the count 0-2, he threw me a curve ball that I hit out of the park and onto an adjoining field. We won the game 7-3 and went on to win the state title the next game. Later that evening, most of the team, our coaches, family and friends came to our house to celebrate the day's events. It was great being able to share my "best" day with teammates, friends and family."

Advice to kids

"If you want to be better than the rest you have to be prepared to work harder than the rest. Preparing yourself to be good enough to play college or professional baseball requires a commitment that many talk about but few make. The hours of practice, working out and preparation can only be managed if you truly love the game. I do not think it is possible for you to make this commitment if you are playing because your dad wants you to, or because you happen to have good hand-eye coordination for a young player. You must love the game. You don't have to love the game to enjoy it. You don't have to love the game to play for your high school team. But if you want to be the best you will need to work harder than you ever believed possible. That will only happen if you love the game.

Also, you must do well in school. Nothing is sadder than knowing players who could not continue to play because their grades were bad. There is no excuse for poor grades. Poor grades mean you have not made an effort - which is a bad habit to get into.

Finally, have a plan. No matter what it is you are doing, have a plan. This will keep you focused and on track."

Senior year statistics
- .536 batting average
- 12 home runs
- 60 RBIs
- 18 stolen bases
- 1.130 slugging percentage

Awards
- National Player of the Week by USA Today in 2003
- USA Today All-American
- Co-MVP of the Nike All-American game
- Gatorade Player of the Year for New Jersey
- Named to several All-American teams

Above/Top: Eric plays third base for the Gulf Coast Yankees of the Gulf Coast League. Bottom-Left: Eric with his brother Aaron and parents Hal and Marsha on graduation day. Bottom-Right: Eric with a group of friends visiting Yankee Stadium.

Left Page/Left: Eric snags a line drive during a high school game his senior year. Right: Eric at bat for the Gulf Coast Yankees.

LUBANSKI

Pennsylvania

First-round pick of 2003 Major League Baseball Draft by Kansas City

Q: What was your best high school baseball moment?

"I was very fortunate to have many memorable baseball experiences during high school. Playing varsity as a freshman, having a great coach like Steve Carcarey who really helped me on and off the field, two league MVP awards, and competing on two USA national teams (the Youth team in 2001 and the Junior National team in 2002) were all amazing. The biggest highlight of my high school career was being selected as the Gatorade National High School Baseball Player of the Year in 2003. The award not only recognized my baseball accomplishments but my efforts in the classroom and community too. Plus, being a Northeast kid, winning this award was pretty special when you consider all the great talent across the country. I think something like over 400,000 players compete in high school baseball, so winning this award was a huge honor."

Chris Lubanski

Kennedy-Kenrick High School
Norristown, Pennsylvania

Date of Birth: March 24, 1985
Height: 6'3"
Weight: 200 lbs.

Bats: left
Throws:

Advice to kids

"Work harder than anyone else, listen to your coaches, and take advantage of all the baseball opportunities you can find. Nothing beats playing the game a lot and I tried to practice nearly every single day during my high school years. Since I starting playing little league, I easily have taken over a million swings so I think you need to work on it everyday you can. I never let any hurdles stand in my way. It gets cold here in

Pennsylvania, we don't have great weather year round to play ball. So you have to do other things to improve. I would do sprints in the snow, hit baseballs in my basement against a couple old mattresses, skip rope in the backyard - anything to get better. Don't let anyone tell you it isn't possible because I'm an example of what can happen when you work hard, love the game, and overcome challenges along the way. Also, for those players who want to play beyond high school, it is really important to get exposure. Playing in some national tournaments or showcases like Perfect Game USA can really help a player get noticed by college coaches and pro scouts. This is even more important for players in parts of the country where baseball maybe isn't really that big. Lots of players can catch the eye of a coach or scout at these events so it is real helpful to compete at the bigger events if you can."

Senior year statistics
- .528 batting average
- 6 homeruns
- 10 triples
- 36 runs scores
- 20 stolen bases
- USA Today All-American

High school career stats
- 158 hits
- 21 homeruns
- 20 triples
- 54 stolen bases
- 134 RBIs

Other
Chris was selected Arizona League's Top Prospect by league managers after batting .326 in his first professional season with the Kansas City Royals in June 2003.

Above/Top: Chris is introduced to Hall Of Fame manager Tommy LaSorda before high school game at Latshaw-McCarthey Field. Bottom: Chris with Royals' Scouting Director Deric Ladnier moments after Chris signed with Kansas City.

Left Page/Top: Chris addresses high school student body after being selected Gatorade National Player Of The Year. Bottom: Chris gets some helpful tips at Kauffman Stadium from Jeff Pentland, Royals' Major League hitting instructor, the day he signed his first pro contract.

Q. What was your most clutch performance and how did you handle the situation.

"My most clutch performance was when I played for the USA Junior National Team at the International Baseball Federation World Championships in 2002. I had two hits against China in the semifinals but Team USA came up a little short and we lost that game. It was a tough loss for us since we had won the Gold Medal the year before when I competed on the Youth National Team. Our loss to China at the Junior tournament meant we couldn't win the Gold, but we still had the opportunity to bring home the Bronze.

We played for the Bronze Medal against Canada. Canada had a very good team led by first round draft selection Adam Loewen. We were disappointed about our loss a day earlier against China, but we knew we had a battle ahead against Canada. Canada took a 1-0 lead early, and then shut us down for six innings. The USA Junior National program had won something like twenty consecutive medals in international competition up to this tournament, so we were only a few innings away from going home with

no medal and breaking the streak. I was leading off our half of the sixth inning, and knew time was starting to slip away. I remember being intensely focused at the plate. There were loud chants of "USA, USA" in the stands, but I just concentrated on seeing the ball real well. I wanted to drive it into the gap so I could get into scoring position. We were playing for our nation and it was crunch time, and I was determined to get on base somehow. I was able to turn on a pretty good fastball, and ended up putting it over the right-centerfield fence for a home run, tying the score 1-1! The home run jump-started the team, and all the guys went on a hitting frenzy over the next couple innings. I ended up hitting my second home run of the game

in the eighth inning, and Team USA went on to capture the Bronze Medal. Winning a second medal in two years for Team USA was a tremendous accomplishment for many of my team-mates and I, and hitting that first home run to tie the score in the Bronze Medal game was a moment I'll never forget."

Above/Top: Chris with brothers Mike and Joe, dad Wally, and friends from Missouri on his first visit to Kansas City as a new Royal. Middle: Chris takes first BP session in Kansas City. Bottom: Chris signs his first professional contract, at Kansas City's Kauffman Stadium, June 11, 2003.

Left Page/Top: Chris is honored as a high school All-American in pregame ceremonies in the spring of 2003. Bottom: Chris with mom, Betsy, dad and high school coach Steve Carcary (far left) being interviewed by media moments before being picked by the Royals, June 3 2003.

DANKS

Texas

First-round pick of 2003 Major League Baseball Draft by Texas

Q: What was your best high school baseball moment?

"It is hard to pick just one "best" moment in high school baseball for me, but just the playoffs in general my senior year would have to be the best time I've ever had in baseball. My high school was ranked No. 1 in the state and nation according to Baseball America so there was, a lot of hype going into the playoffs. Also the whole school became fired up for the baseball team and wanted to take part in everything. It was like football season in the spring. No matter where we played there was a large following, and in some cases the school chartered buses to allow as many students as possible to show up. And then the last week of my high school baseball career was the week of my graduation, major league baseball draft, and the state tournament, so if you don't think there was a lot of excitement and just stuff going on then you are wrong. But by far the 2003 5A playoffs was the best time I've ever had."

John Danks

Round Rock High School
Round Rock, Texas

Date of Birth: April 15, 1985
Height: 6'2"
Weight: 195 lbs.
Bats: left
Throws: left

P i t c h e r

Senior year statistics

- .404 batting average
- 1.3 ERA
- 173 strikeouts
- 100 innings pitched
- 2 home runs
- 45 stolen bases
- Named USA Today All-American

Advice to kids

"The advice I would give a young kid with aspirations to play college and/or professional baseball would be to just keep working hard and don't give up. You have to believe in yourself before anyone else does. Never in my wildest dreams would I have imagined myself picked ninth overall in the Major League Draft. Going into my junior year I hadn't received a letter from any colleges, so I just figured I would be a pretty good high school player and do what most guys do and go get a degree and be done with baseball. But I wanted to give myself every opportunity to make it to the next level just so when I looked back I would know I did everything I could to make it to the next level. Fortunately with the grace of God I worked hard enough to make it, but had I not I wouldn't be anywhere with baseball. With all that said, hard work and confidence are the keys to making it in baseball."

Above/Top: John pitching at Dell Diamond during the 2003 playoffs. Bottom: John sitting in Grady Fuson's box watching the Rangers warm upon his signing day.

Left Page/Left:: John with Orel Hershiser. Right: John with his mother, Renee, at the airport the day he left for Arizona for the beginning of pro ball.

Q. What was your most clutch performance and how did you handle the situation.

"My most clutch moment would have to be in the Texas 5A State Championship game. We played Elkins High School out of Houston. They were the defending state and national champions. I gave up five runs in the first three innings and dug us a 5-0 hole, but from the fourth inning on I didn't give up another hit and gave us a chance to win the game. Although we lost 5-4, I feel I kept my composure and did what I had to do. Even though most of the

game is a blur and I've tried my hardest to forget that day, I would have to say I just took on a "bulldog" attitude and put the first three innings behind me and focused

more and more on every pitch, and that is how I was able to stay focused and put in my "clutch" effort."

Above: John pitching in a playoff game at Dell Diamond in the 2003 season.

Left Page/Top-Right: John with his sister Emily and brother Jordan standing in front of the Rangers' spring training facility in Surprise, Arizona.

Top-Left: John pitching in a playoff game at Baylor University in 2003. Bottom: John tries on his new cap at a Rangers press conference at the Ballpark in Arlington on July 11, 2003.

About the Author

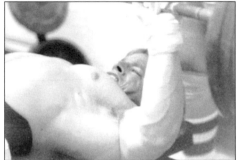

Steve Knight

Photos by Kim Ross

A pioneer in the field of mental preparation
for tournament competition, Steve Knight is a 4x State and 2x National
Powerlifting champion, and current Oregon state record holder in the
squat at 722 lbs.

Steve's confidence building techniques and distraction management routines are transforming the way coaches and athletes prepare for competition. The core of Steve's system is perspective: Confidence is a skill, not a genetic gift.

Founder of Let's Win! Publishing, Steve resides in Portland, Ore., and is currently pursing a degree at Portland State University.

ORDER THE BOOK

The Players' Guide
to Competitive Confidence

winningstate.com

WinningSTATE–BASEBALL

Lets Win! Publishing
1110 SW Clay #43
Portland, OR 97201
503.224.8252